Tarot

A UNIVERSAL LANGUAGE

Experiencing the Road of Life through Symbols

"The explanations are clear and useful for the beginning tarot reader and those looking for a quick refresher course. She not only defines the energy of the cards but shows the reader how to deal with reversals in positive and proactive ways. I loved the fact that I could start using the tarot card readings right away. A must-have book for the person who loves to learn by doing and does not want to wait a year to begin exploring the tarot first hand. Useful information on numerology and symbolism in general.

—Happy Customer.
California

"This is by far the best basic book on Tarot I have ever read. It is organized very clearly and each card is explained thoroughly. Great for beginners and more advanced Tarot readers."

—Sally
Iowa

"Tarot: A Universal Language is the finest tarot book I have ever used. Excellent for beginners as well as advanced tarot readers. The interpretations of each card are clear, concise, and positive. The symbology glossary assists in the educational process and accuracy of readings. This book has changed my life. I highly recommend it!"

—Leslie
Michigan

"I consider Beatrex Quntanna the premier expert on Tarot. Her exceptional background in symbology and numerology as well as her extraordinary psychic insight makes this book unique among Tarot books and a must have reference for the tarot novice and professional alike. This is the ONLY Tarot book I recommend for my students."

—Janet Lightstone
founder, Lightstone Academy of
Psychic Arts & Lightstone Source

contents

HOW TO USE THIS BOOK

This book is organized into sections explaining how to prepare for a reading, pulling the cards, asking questions and interpreting the cards that are pulled, what their positions mean, what changes when cards are reversed, and what the details for each card symbolize. Refer to the Symbols section, beginning on page 51, for an in-depth explanation of each card and its symbols.

A good place to start is the Preparing for a Reading section (page 134), where you can choose the type of reading that is best for your present situation. The easier readings (Bedtime, Card a Day, General Info, Yes/No, Daily, Weekly Forecast) are described on pages 135 through 139. Follow the instructions for spreading out the cards. Turn the cards right side up and use the Major (page 7) and/or Minor Arcana (page 19) sections to find the interpretation of each card. Read the explanation and identify the particular meaning that speaks to you in the moment.

When first learning Tarot, it is a good idea to review the quality of each suit of the Minor Arcana. An overview of the personality cards begins on page 76. These qualities are defined at the beginning of each section of the suits. Learning the numerological values is helpful for additional understanding. Numerological interpretations begin on page 18.

As you continue to use this book to interpret the cards you pull in your reading, you will eventually learn the meaning of each card and begin to develop your own glossary as you apply the meaning of each card to your life experience.

CHOOSING YOUR TAROT DECK

There are many different Tarot decks available. Look through the selection of Tarot decks on display at your local bookstore and notice the deck that excites you or stimulates your interest. The one that seems to give you the most visual pleasure is the deck that is yours.

Many people collect Tarot decks and have as many as twelve, or more different decks. As you become more familiar with the Tarot, one or another of the many available decks will become "your" deck.

All decks consist of 78 cards; 22 Major Arcana cards and 56 Minor Arcana cards. The Minor Arcana cards are divided into four suits: Wands, Swords, Cups and Pentacles. Pentacles are also often referred to as Coins. A few decks have other names for the four suits, but they all correspond to the standard suits, For example, in the Voyager Tarot deck the suit of Swords is called Crystals and the suit of Pentacles is called Worlds.

The illustrations in this book are from the Rider-Waite Tarot deck. If you are new to Tarot, you may want to start with this deck as it is one of the most widely used and most popular and its symbols speak a very clear language.

CARE & TREATMENT OF YOUR CARDS

Remember, your deck is a source of wise council, an Oracle. Treat your cards with respect. According to tradition, it is best to keep your cards in cotton or silk or in a special box. Many Tarot readers collect fabric, boxes, and silk bags for their decks.

When you first open your deck, greet the cards one at a time and let your energy blend with each card as if you were passing through a receiving line at a very important party. You might even want to say a special blessing or prayer as you work with your deck for the first time. You might ask that this deck blend with you and your highest purpose, so that your cards can be used for truth and honesty in observation of self and others.

When you have a new deck, it works best to carry it with you at all times for the first month or so. This gives the deck a chance to match itself with your vibrations and your life, thus enhancing the energy exchange you need and want from your cards.

When using your cards, fan them out face down on a table. Use the palms of both hands to mix them well; turning them in various directions so they form a "pool of consciousness" in front of you. This form of mixing holds the energy in the cards and keeps your cards in better condition, while the standard form of shuffling should only be used to dispel negative energy from your cards.

MAJOR ARCANA

The word "arcana" means secret doctrine. Secrets have always aroused curiosity in man and inspired succeeding generations to continue to seek the truth.

The Major Arcana of the Tarot consists of the first 22 cards of the 78 cards of the full Tarot deck. The cards are numbered 0 through 21. They are the most potent cards in the deck and are a model of Wholeness.

To clearly view this Model of Wholeness, place your Major Arcana cards in numerical order beginning with The Fool card (0). Place The Fool card in the center at the top of the layout area and then set out three rows of seven cards per row, as shown below.

THE FOOL

First Row: Numbers 1 through 7
(The Magician through The Chariot)

Second Row: Numbers 8 through 14
(Strength through Temperance)

Third Row: Numbers 15 through 21
(The Devil through The World)

Each row represents a stage in man's development:

• Row 1 indicates the synthesis of Consciousness into Life

• Row 2 shows the development of personality

• Row 3 integrates consciousness and personality (individual expression) as it manifests in the world.

The Fool is the floater card. I prefer to place it on top of the tableau as it represents the involvement of the super-consciousness, promoting the potential, and motivating the promise of the evolution of wholeness. The Fool card is the umbrella over the entire deck. It is the atmosphere or climate that exists within us to induce experiences in life.

The Major Arcana cards single out a stage of development on the spectrum of wholeness. The process begins with The Fool card (the promise of things to come) and ends with The World card (potential actualized), thus completing the promise promoted by The Fool.

Each Major card has a law and a lesson reflecting the values of our times and promoting the evolution of experience on the internal and external planes of awareness. The law is what you have to learn while travelling here. The lesson is the experience which allows the law to be learned. In the following descriptions of the Major Arcana cards, the laws are shown in all capital letters. For example, The Hierophant (5) is the Law of Tradition. It asks us to look at what tradition is — a reflection of our sociological, economical, and moral values and used as a basis of evaluation during the time period in which we live. The lesson is to experience whether the interpretation of this tradition is accurate for us.

Reversals are cards that are upside down to you as you read the cards. This is true whether you are reading for yourself or for someone else since the cards are always laid out for the reader, the person interpreting the cards. The qualities listed under the Reversed heading are merely showing you the inner place and inner work that is needed in your development.

THE FOOL.

THE FOOL – 0

POTENTIAL
- The promise of things to come
  The energy you are bringing into yourself in the moment
- A leap of faith
- A new beginning
- A "go-for-it" attitude
- Accessing your potential (not caring if you look foolish)—
  Remember, the guy with the lampshade
  on his head may be having more fun than you
- Willing to play full out
- Going through life lightheartedly.

REVERSED:
- Unwilling to take risks
- No faith in yourself
- Worry
- Holding yourself back
- Being afraid of looking foolish
- Afraid to "let go and let God"
- No faith to take the leap
- Taking life too seriously.

THE MAGICIAN.

THE MAGICIAN – I

TALENT
- Ability to convert from the ethereal to
  the physical
- Masculine polarity in its purest form
- All things are possible for you
- Having all the tools for success
- Time to focus your intention and attention
- A man who symbolizes every woman's fantasy

REVERSED:
- Misuse of power
- A master of illusion
- Seeing everything as impossible
- Lacking self-confidence
- Doubting your ability to manifest or create
- Not accessing your tools (talent).

MAJOR ARCANA

THE HIGH PRIESTESS – II

INTUITION
- The Feminine polarity in its purest form
- Purity

REVERSED:
- Not trusting your intuition
- Overriding intuition with logic
- Diluting your femininity
- Prostituting yourself
- Selling yourself short
- Ask, "What intuitive hit am I not listening to?"

THE EMPRESS – III

LOVE
- The epitome of the Natural Woman
- Fertility
- Nurturance
- The ability to get your needs met
- Flowing with what feels natural
- Knowing how to take care of yourself and others
- Being touchable, lovable and nurturing
- The perfect wife/mother
- Creativity at its best

REVERSED:
- Not nurturing self or others
- A poor self-image manifests in feeling unloved
- Ask, "What do I want in order to get my needs met?"
- Do for yourself rather than expect others to do for you. Remember, you can only be loved to the extent you love yourself.

THE EMPEROR – IV

SUCCESS
- Ability to respond to success and manifest in the outside world
- The perfect husband/father
- Successful in business
- Structured, logical, and grounded
- Having a foundation for success
- "Chairman of the Board" type

REVERSED:
- Not assuming responsibility—in the world, in a relationship, in business.
- Disorganized
- A social dropout
- Unable to work the system for success in the world
- Disconnected
- Rebellious against the system
- A man who has turned his back on a woman

THE HIEROPHANT – V

TRADITION
- The authority figure
- The bridge between humanity and divinity
- The teacher's teacher
- The interpreter of life (teacher, lawyer, therapist, preacher, rabbi, doctor) through listening and reflection
- Seeking interpretation through traditions, social awareness, church, dogma, society's rules.
- Needing advice and interpretation through the eyes of an authority.

REVERSED:
- Learning to interpret life for yourself
- Breaking away from tradition, dogma, ritual, church, society's rules
- Learning to live by using your own intuition and becoming your own authority
- Knowing there is more to life than what meets the eye
- Seeing beyond the physical.

THE LOVERS – VI

RELATIONSHIP
- Integration of the masculine and feminine life energy
- Perfect inner balance of the masculine and feminine principles
- Union of opposites
- Healthy relationship
- Commitment
- Marriage
- Good health

REVERSED:
- Broken partnerships
- Selfishness
- Love for all the wrong reasons
- Divorce
- Separation
- Bad health
- Lack of commitment

THE CHARIOT – VII

ACTION
- Taking action for victory in life
- Broad, sweeping changes
- Positioning yourself for success
- Take action now to move forward in life

REVERSED:
- Upheaval in your life from not taking action
- Putting your foot on the brakes when it needs to be on the gas pedal

STRENGTH – VIII

PASSION

- Understanding the dynamics of the beauty and the beast within
- Learning to express your higher and lower selves without judgement
- Integrating consciousness with the physical, thereby creating a passion for life

REVERSED:

- Denial of natural expression
- Giving power away to your lower forces
- Out of control
- Stubborn

THE HERMIT – IX

INDIVIDUALITY

- Knowing yourself as an individual
- Recognizing your inner qualities
- Your God-self uniqueness manifests your inner light
- Time to take your spirituality off the mountaintop and shine your light out into the world

REVERSED:

- Contemplating and observing
- Hiding out and retreating from life
- Denying your own individuality
- Not sharing your knowledge; keeping it to yourself. Caution: Do not stay on the mountaintop too long!

THE WHEEL OF FORTUNE – X

LIFE LESSON
- In time and on time with your life's blueprint
- The drum of destiny beats in your favor.
- Experiencing good fortune

REVERSED:
- Denying your destiny
- Taken off of your path
- Everything is out of synch
- Denial of life lessons
- Getting stuck in feeling sorry for yourself
- Misfortune

JUSTICE – XI

KARMA
- Activating the laws of Cause and Effect (Every action has a reaction; what you put out you get back.)
- Expect compensation for actions taken
- Actions now get equalized and balanced
- Winning a lawsuit.

REVERSED:
- Not accepting responsibility for your actions
- Being forced to face what you do not want to see
- Blaming others rather than seeing the balance of action
- Feeling as if an injustice has been done.

THE HANGED MAN – XII

DETACHMENT
- Learning to accept rather than control.
- Taking time out to reflect.
- Being willing to "hang out" and do nothing.
- Being calm in the midst of the storm.

REVERSED:
- Clinging to the past.
- Living life through a rear view mirror.
- Not willing to change.
- Afraid to just hang out and observe.
- Trying to control.
- Being a martyr.

DEATH – XIII

TRANSFORMATION
- There is no compromise – change is imminent
- Make a clean break
- Time to let go of the past.
- Rejuvenation
- Regeneration
- New beginnings

REVERSED:
- The Universe has you on hold.
- Delays are appropriate.
- Do not personalize the feeling of "stuckness."

TEMPERANCE – XIV

BALANCE
- Experimentation and modification.
- This is a time of learning to manage life by blending extremes, knowing boundaries, and setting limits.
- Inner and outer congruity is very important now.
- Know what it takes to keep yourself centered.

REVERSED:
- Life is unmanageable.
- Moderation is needed.
- Obsessive and compulsive behaviors are causing imbalance.
- Could indicate poor health, exhaustion, or stress.
- Out of alignment with spiritual and physical realities.
- Time to set limits and boundaries.

THE DEVIL – XV

CONFINEMENT
- Feeling confined, constricted, limited.
- 360 degree test with 180 degree vision – you are only seeing half of the picture.
- Options required.
- Ask, "How many different ways can I look at this situation?"

REVERSED:
- The light at the end of the tunnel appears.
- The testing period is over.
- The road to freedom has been found.
- You have seen your options.
- The solution to your problem has been found.

THE TOWER – XVI

SPONTANEITY
- Learning to live in the moment
- An unexpected event leads you into freedom
- Do not put anything off until tomorrow
- Do whatever is appropriate in the moment
- Clear the way so new consciousness can appear.

REVERSED:
- Resisting change.
- Staying stuck by trying to control the outcome.
- Refusing to go with the flow.

THE STAR – XVII

NEW DIRECTIONS
- Breakthrough to a new level of consciousness.
- On track
- Golden opportunities on the horizon
- Support coming from higher sources to provide guidance and direction

REVERSED:
- Search for inner direction rather than outer guideposts
- A missed opportunity
- Ask, "Where am I being thrown off course and not willing to accept a new level of consciousness?"

THE MOON – XVIII

FEARS AND PHOBIAS
- A time to face up to and look at what you keep hidden from yourself.
- A warning to stay on the path and avoid outside influences of negativity.
- Being deceived or deceiving yourself.
- Absorbing toxic or poisonous energy; i.e., drugs or alcohol. Drug or alcohol abuse. Time to face your darker side and bring it into the light.

REVERSED:
- A warning of personal safety.
- Danger in the dark.
- Doing anything to avoid facing the truth.
- Secrets, lies, deception, depression, and repression.
- Denial
- Cheating
- Illegal activities

THE SUN – XIX

ENLIGHTENMENT
- The source of energy
- Happiness
- Abundance
- Success
- Prosperity
- Fulfillment
- Playfulness
- The child-ego state revealed

REVERSED:
- Not seeing that all is available to you.
- Ask, "Where am I denying myself happiness?"
- Your dimmer switch is turning down the sunlight!

JUDGEMENT – XX

FREEDOM

- Freedom from judgement.
- A clean slate is now available, a new life on a new level of consciousness.
- Congratulations! You have let go and integrated beyond black/white, right/wrong, good/bad and have moved into a more integrated version of yourself.

REVERSED:

- Being your own worst enemy
- Judging yourself constantly
- Beating yourself up
- Making yourself wrong
- Afraid of what people think
- Feeling guilty
- Low self-esteem
- Stop punishing yourself for past deeds and let go.

THE WORLD – XXI

ATTAINMENT

- Unlimited opportunity for success
- Attainment
- Having it all
- Your full potential realized
- Victory in life
- Mastery of the inner and outer planes of awareness
- Acknowledge your accomplishments.

REVERSED:

- Fear of failure
- Not willing to take responsibility for success
- A loser attitude
- Never bringing anything to completion.
- Feeling defeated
- Walking to the door of success and saying, "Oh well, it wouldn't have worked, anyway."

mInOR ARCAnA

The Minor Arcana teach us how to play the Game of Life on four levels and provide us with an inter-dimensional view of ourselves.

Envision the Minors as a game of Life played on four game boards at once. It is based on a system of numbers and areas, or levels, of learning indicated by each suit; Wands, Cups, Swords, and Pentacles. Wands symbolize learning on the spiritual level, Cups symbolize learning on the emotional level, Swords symbolize learning on the mental level, and Pentacles symbolize learning on a physical level. Additional details are found in the in-depth sections on each of the suits.

The energy pattern used to understand each area of learning is defined by the number on the card (Ace through 10). The numbers in the Minor Arcana give a value to the learning pattern, thus describing the formula to be used in identifying and solving issues. Numbers show us "the way in" and "the way out" of any given situation. They provide us with a greater understanding of the equivalents of energy to be used in life.

The system I have chosen to use to define the Minor Arcana is based on Numerology. The numerical definition of each numbered Minor Arcana card is combined with the meaning of the suit to arrive at a definition. Let's use the Ace of Wands as an example. All Aces relate to the number 1. One (1) means new beginnings, individuality, and originality. The Suit of Wands indicates the area of spiritual learning and inspiration. Therefore, the interpretation of the Ace of Wands is new beginnings on your spiritual path. Another interpretation could be individual and original ideas motivating you to new spiritual growth.

NUMEROLOGY INTERPRETATIONS

#	INTERPRETATION
1	Individuality – originality – uniqueness REVERSED: Dependency – following the crowd
2	Duality – working with heart and head and learning to balance both so that decisions can be made REVERSED: Off balance – indecisive
3	Creativity – having fun – being social – good self-esteem REVERSED: Ego investment – creative block – poor self-esteem
4	System for success in the world—A logical look at how to develop your plan for success. REVERSED: Illogical – unstructured – ungrounded
5	Change – variety – expansion REVERSED: "Stuck-ness"
6	Love – health – relationships – commitment – home – service REVERSED: Lack of commitment – being taken advantage of
7	Lesson time – Learn to look at the bigger picture – Do not get stuck in the details. REVERSED: Obsession – over-analysis
8	Money – power – manifestation REVERSED: Fear of failure or success - Not knowing what you want
9	Spiritual accent – talk to the Universe – Look to see where you can shine your light. REVERSED: Drained – emotional – overly-sensitive
10	New beginnings that set you up for the future. REVERSED: Not willing to complete a process.

WANDS

Wands symbolize the Fire element and the Spiritual plane. They indicate the spiritual world, which provides enlightenment, inspiration, progress, and growth. Wands promote the ability to be inspired and go for greater glory. Wands also indicate career progress. Wands people are inspirational, growth-oriented, charismatic, fiery, and explosive.

ACE of WANDS.

ACE

QUALITIES

- A new career opportunity
- Growth
- Progress
- Spiritual development
- All things possible
- A new inspiration that will motivate movement on your spiritual path.

REVERSED

- Having a hard time grasping a new beginning
- Denial
- Turning away from an opportunity to grow

TWO

QUALITIES

- A decision is being made in your favor concerning growth, career, or spiritual path
- A new view providing balance through the use of your intuition to see choices that are available regarding career and spiritual development.

REVERSED

- Indecisiveness
- Lack of vision
- Stuck in the mental process
- Intuitive input denied
- Unable to reach a decision
- The time may be inappropriate for decision-making; all options are not in yet.
- Blocked vision regarding career/spiritual path
- "Windshield wipers of the mind" effect (going back and forth, feeling unbalanced)
- Follow your heart not your head in making decisions regarding growth and/or career.
- Feeling defeated
- Walking to the door of success and saying, "Oh well, it wouldn't have worked, anyway."

THREE

QUALITIES

- Time to have fun and be creative with your growth process or career
- Creative talent may emerge now through career opportunities
- Career choice must be fun
- Creativity emerging
- Perhaps time to turn a hobby into a career
- Manifesting good self-esteem in lifestyle, growth potential, and career.

REVERSED

- Poor self-esteem
- Not having any fun in life, in work, or in spiritual growth.
- Ego problems at work
- Look for feelings of insecurity
- Find out what makes you feel good and pursue it.
- Hiding from your talent because of poor self-esteem
- Worrying unnecessarily
- Time to schedule more fun time into your life.

FOUR

QUALITIES

- Your foundation for success is now set.
- Growth, progress, and career are established and managed to perfection.
- Good management at work; happy work environment, happy life environment.
- Potential marriage

REVERSED

- Poor management at work
- New structure required
- Logical plan needed
- Re-evaluation needed
- Turnover in the corporate structure
- New foundations need to be applied and follow-through is required.
- Follow the plan!
- Feeling ungrounded as if the floor has just caved in.
- No ground of being
- Trouble with management at work.
- Being effected by poor management at work.
- Transfer of power

FIVE

QUALITIES
- Expansion taking place
- Spiritual growth in process
- A variety of opportunities available
- Take action, move forward, and move fast.
- Expanding at a rapid pace; may be necessary to move in many directions at once.
- A breakthrough has occurred giving you freedom of expansion. Go for it!
- Change/expansion in career
- Work-related travel

REVERSED
- Feeling stuck, constricted, confined, chaotic
- Putting on the brakes
- Feeling as if your wheels are spinning and going nowhere fast; ready to leave the starting gate, but the gate is closed.
- Going every which way but forward

SIX

QUALITIES
- Receiving recognition for a job well done
- Commitment and love are the successful ingredients in the work that you do spiritually or career-wise.
- Career opportunities available in the areas of health, beauty, interior design, home and service to others. (For instance, nursing, health practitioner, makeup artist, catering, real estate, etc.).
- Being recognized for dedication and commitment to the job.
- You may be up for a promotion at work.
- You are loving your career and committed to it.

REVERSED
- Lack of commitment on the job
- Unhappiness
- No personal satisfaction because of lack of commitment
- Someone may be trying to take advantage of you to serve their own purposes.
- Unhealthy attitude about life
- Missing your higher purpose by taking a job you do not love.

mɪnor arcana-wands

SEVEN

QUALITIES
- Genius is at work.
- The lessons required to turn wisdom into knowledge have been learned.
- The learning process is now deeply ingrained and will lead to manifestation.
- Lessons have been learned through hard work.
- The big picture of life and career is now realized.
- The analytical, logical, and detailed mind is working and combining itself with creativity to provide the best of all things.

REVERSED
- Letting the details get you down
- Over-perfectionism
- Picking over details - picky, picky, picky! Picayune
- Over-detailed
- Losing sight of the big picture
- Getting stuck in the small view
- Obsessing mentally
- Trying too hard
- Missing the mark
- Self-sabotage
- Not wanting to complete the project.
- Not wanting to learn the lesson because you will have to apply it.
- Making life too difficult.
- Stuck on learning rather than experiencing.

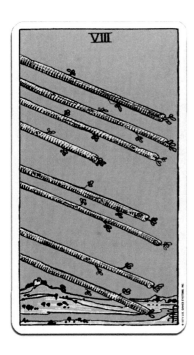

EIGHT

QUALITIES
- Harvesting the fruits of labors
- Manifestation in a very powerful way
- Getting what you want out of life and career
- Goals realized

REVERSED
- Lack of commitment on the job
- Manifestation is at hand
- Clarify what you want for yourself, spiritually, in your career and in your life style.
- Knowing what you want is the key to manifesting—visualize yourself receiving it. Write it down, say it out loud and it will happen.

NINE

QUALITIES

- Spiritual fulfillment
- A completion within
- Ready to go out into the world and make a difference
- This is the card of the humanitarian
- An audience awaits you
- Take your light from within, out to the masses and shine.
- Ready to accomplish your spiritual mission.

REVERSED

- Drained
- Taking care of others' needs before your own
- Supersensitive at work
- Anxiety attacks
- Emotionalism
- Loss of self
- Loss of individuality
- Time to step back and take care of yourself

TEN

QUALITIES

- New beginnings spiritually and at work
- Hard work pays off, setting in a new future on a new level
- Acknowledge the job well done
- Complete and move on to the next phase of evolution.

REVERSED

- Afraid to let go and move on
- Not letting go of the past
- Not completing the project in order to avoid moving forward
- Blocked vision
- Look to see what is being put off to avoid a new beginning
- Completion is in order
- Let your future unfold before you

PAGE of WANDS.

PAGE

QUALITIES
- A younger person adds to growth and progress through inspiration
- Being open to a new attitude in your career
- Pages bring inspiration, illumination, and energy into life showing readiness to grow and bloom into a new kind of power.

REVERSED
- Immature attitudes in relation to career, growth, or education
- This person is uninspired by life
- Has a tendency to implode anger
- No vision for the future
- Lacks direction

KNIGHT of WANDS.

KNIGHT

QUALITIES
- A forward movement in spirituality and enlightenment in career.
- Possibility of getting a promotion or someone coming into your life to guide your progress.

REVERSED
- Someone in your environment is holding you back and sabotaging efforts to move forward
- Being passed over for a promotion
- This person keeps you from growing

QUEEN of WANDS.

QUEEN

QUALITIES
- A people-oriented person
- Ms. Personality-plus
- Charismatic
- A spiritual leader
- Growth-oriented
- Inspiring
- Energetic
- Visible

REVERSED
- Imploded anger
- Could have a tendency to lose her temper
- Scattering of energy
- Bossy/snobby
- Stuck in her ego
- Misusing spiritual principles
- Frazzled
- Unkempt
- Disillusioned

KING of WANDS.

KING

QUALITIES
- Leader
- Charismatic
- Igniting
- Politician
- Inspirational
- Growth-oriented
- Chairman of the Board
- Leader of causes
- Guru-type
- Community organizer
- Empowers others
- Dynamic, creative, energetic man

REVERSED
- Hothead
- Overbearing
- Stuck in the ego
- Negative attitude
- Puts fear into everyone around him
- Could be a person demoted or who just lost a good position
- Denial of power
- Controlling
- Burned out
- Loss of energy

CUPS

Cups symbolize the Water element. They connect you to your Soul's expression of love and feelings, the Emotional plane. Cups speak to the depths of the emotional self, the heart's desire, how you love and are loved. Creative expression is resourced out of the Suit of Cups and brings forth fulfillment in life. Cups people are emotional, creative, loving, and receptive.

ACE of CUPS.

ACE

QUALITIES

- New beginnings in love
- A new sense of self
- A new identity in loving self
- A new creative process that will bring on fulfillment in self-expression
- The beginning of a grand love affair.

REVERSED

- Denial
- False gaiety
- Unhappiness
- Not allowing new love to enter your life
- Blocked feelings

TWO

QUALITIES

- Two energies coming together to generate love in harmony and balance
- Chemistry; the beginning of a passionate love affair; the intoxication of love.
- A decision being made around love in your favor.

REVERSED

- An unhealthy relationship
- Breakup of a relationship
- Not the right time to make a decision around love
- No passion

THREE

QUALITIES
- Celebration
- Being social
- Having fun
- Letting the little kid out
- Being creative

REVERSED
- Poor self-esteem in love issues
- Feeling worthless
- Ego in the way, blocking the emotions.
- Feeling depressed about life and love.
- Taking love too seriously

FOUR

QUALITIES
- The foundation is being set for a love relationship.
- Allow yourself to see what is being offered.
- Potential for letting past expressions of love get in the way of the new foundation that is being set
- The tree of happiness is available—don't miss this opportunity!

REVERSED
- Logic gets in the way of feelings.
- Crying over spilt milk from past relationships
- Missing the opportunity of new love being offered
- Set plans for successful emotional expression so needs can be met in love.
- A time to heal past relationships.

FIVE

QUALITIES

- Qualities
- A change and/or expansion of love
- A relationship growing to a new level
- Leaving an old relationship behind
- A change of lover or spouse
- Taking a romantic trip
- Time to move ahead, even if it means leaving someone behind.
- Opening to a variety of love expressions

REVERSED

- Not willing to make changes where they are needed in love
- Stuck in a rut
- Dependency on love that does not work
- Wishing to change a relationship and not having the guts to do it
- Standing still can be stifling at this level.

SIX

QUALITIES

- Love commitment
- Good, healthy love relationship
- Love without fear
- A happy home
- A meeting with childhood sweetheart or a renewal of love from earlier years.

REVERSED

- Being taken advantage of in love
- No commitment
- Unhealthy relationship
- Not getting your needs met and not knowing how to ask for what you want.

SEVEN

QUALITIES
- Lessons learned around love
- Time to look at the broader picture
- Do not let the details get you down
- Time to reconnect with fantasies and dreams and create a broader perspective around feelings.

REVERSED
- Obsession
- Over-analyzing
- Psychological warfare
- Picky! Picky! Picky!
- Seeing the negative in your partner
- Letting the details "get you down"
- Being critical
- Critically obsessing over your partner
- Being too mental
- Learning lessons around love the hard way
- Repeating the same lessons over and over again

EIGHT

QUALITIES
- Manifestation of great love
- Being willing to go for what you want and actually getting it
- New relationships on the horizon

REVERSED
- Time to clarify what you want to manifest in love.
- Make a list of all of the characteristics you desire in a mate and get ready to manifest!

NINE

QUALITIES
- Expressing love through humanitarian efforts
- Contributing to other peoples' lives
- Fulfillment in love
- Sharing love by taking on a cause
- Bringing who you are out to a larger audience by using the expression of Universal Love
- Getting involved in charities/community projects that fulfill a higher need
- Adding the spiritual equation to feelings
- Connecting to a greater source

REVERSED
- Taking care of others' needs before your own
- Creating an emotional drain
- Being tired out
- Being burned out
- Exhaustion
- Being overly sensitive
- Crying all the time
- Needing to take time out to regroup.

TEN

QUALITIES
- A new beginning in love that expands through the future
- A renewal that moves your relationship to a new level
- A completion of one cycle and the beginning of another
- Happiness, frivolity
- Bringing in the cycles of new generations, families
- A cause for celebration
- A recommitment

REVERSED
- Settling for less in love because it is familiar
- Not willing to go the last mile to get over the hump and get into a new beginning
- A sense of stagnation and unwillingness to go any further
- The ending of a relationship that continues to linger in its ending.

PAGE

QUALITIES
- Embracing new attitudes around love
- Falling in love for the first time
- A younger person, perhaps a child, going through the first phases of romantic illusions and fantasies around love
- Remembering the first youthful phases of love in life

REVERSED
- Immature attitudes around love
- Emotional expression needed
- Time to communicate with your children
- Somebody around you having to face reality versus fantasy around love and emotional issues
- Could be the beginning of a drinking or drug problem
- A young person's first experience with romantic rejection

PAGE of CUPS.

KNIGHT

QUALITIES
- Prince Charming has arrived!
- A move and change in the emotional/love process that allows you to receive love from a worthy candidate
- Someone bringing love to you
- Having someone around who loves you very much
- Accepting what is being offered, for it will move you to the next level in development on the emotional plane.

REVERSED
- Being held back by a person who is very depressed around love
- Negative thoughts around love that manipulate you and keep you from getting your needs met
- Possible indication that love partner is no longer interested
- Could be a warning to be cautious where love is concerned
- Emotions being stifled by an outside source.

KNIGHT of CUPS.

QUEEN of CUPS.

QUEEN

QUALITIES
- The Lover's lover
- A tremendous appetite for love, creativity, receptivity, orgasm, heart's desire, ecstasy, and femininity at its best
- A magnet for love
- Takes the line of least resistance
- Likes things the easy way
- Tendency to connect with a man for identity
- An artist, performer, psychic
- Enormously vulnerable
- Tendency to be wishy-washy, deeply sensitive, with a heightened level of emotional awareness
- Verbally expressive
- Ebb and flow, like the tides—goes in and goes out
- Tends to "go with the flow"

REVERSED
- Immature attitudes around love
- Emotional expression needed
- Time to communicate with your children
- Somebody around you having to face reality versus fantasy around love and emotional issues
- Could be the beginning of a drinking or drug problem
- A young person's first experience with romantic rejection

KING of CUPS.

KING

QUALITIES
- Every woman's fantasy
- Romantic man, great lover
- Artistic, creative – may be an actor, poet, or writer
- A man in touch with his feminine side
- The creative dreamer
- Great father/homemaker
- Loves to cook/tend the garden
- Great for a weekend in the mountains or a romantic vacation
- Be sure you can handle the spontaneity before committing to this type of man
- A dream-maker—not necessarily a producer

REVERSED
- Secretive
- Emotionally bottled up
- Deeply brooding
- Manic-depressive
- A man letting his emotions run his life
- His illusions and fantasies have become delusions
- Tendency toward drug abuse, alcoholism, and deception.

SWORDS

Swords symbolize the Air element and the Mental plane. Swords can build you up or tear you down. They are double-edged, indicating the dualistic nature that exists in the mind. They teach offense or defense, encouragement or discouragement. Swords show where you are defining yourself and moving towards your own identity, or where you are giving power away to acquiesce to the needs of others. Swords ask you to have the courage to cut the apron strings of society and family and develop yourself as an individual. Swords are the motivational development of your personal power. Swords people are mental, logical, analytical, and organized.

ACE of SWORDS.

ACE

QUALITIES
- Triumph and victory over authority
- The beginning of a powerful new personal process where all things are possible

REVERSED
- Self-inflicted pain
- Not having the courage to stand up for yourself
- Sabotaging yourself
- Can indicate an identity crisis
- Someone else's opinion of you is more important than your own opinion of yourself.

TWO

QUALITIES
- "Windshield wipers of the mind" - mental obsessing and going back and forth with decision-making. For example, "I don't know"…"yes, I will"…"no, I won't."
- A decision being made in your favor that requires blind faith
- Follow your heart, not your head

REVERSED
- A time to gather facts in the decision-making process
- The mind is in a war zone, obsessing and blocking intuition
- Time to, "let go and let God"
- Not an appropriate time to make a decision—all options are not in yet
- Stuck in logic, ignoring feelings.

mɪɴor ArcAɴA—swords

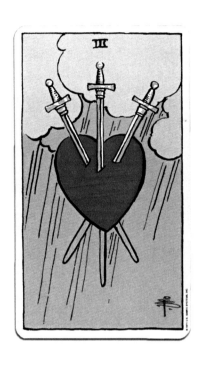

THREE

QUALITIES

- Tremendous heartache
- Self-esteem has been hurt by taking in the inadequacies of another and making them your own
- A need to express feelings in a creative way to allow self-esteem to return and take the javelins of another person's anger and rage out of the heart
- Allowing another person to define you in a painful way
- The mind shutting off the heart and making the heartache worse

REVERSED

- Old pain from early environmental training needs to be looked at and addressed—this pain has been hurting for several years, creating tremendous self-esteem and insecurity issues in life.
- It's a time to look back and review the place & time when the upsets that blocked creative expression for life began, and allow them to heal so that the same repeated pattern does not need to affect how you feel about yourself anymore
- Could indicate self as the cause of pain in someone else's process

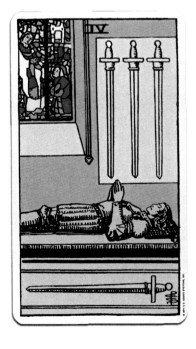

FOUR

QUALITIES

- Time to remove yourself from past pain
- Sleeping on a new identity
- A new identity is available if it is allowed to come to the surface
- Time to decide whether to return to the patterns of past pain or move forward to a new outlook
- Congratulations! You have moved to a place of choice. The pain has been taken out of your heart and provides a new vision that will allow a new format for success in life.

REVERSED

- Falling back into the pain of the Three of Swords
- Blocked vision
- Identity crisis

FIVE

QUALITIES

- Expanding and moving forward—Leaving an old battle behind
- A battle won, opponents defeated
- New strength and vigor to make the changes necessary to advance
- An expanded thought process
- A change of ideas that allows for a variety of new experiences, acknowledging that life can be different
- The atmosphere and climate of life is changing

REVERSED

- Mentally stuck; looking back on old issues; stuck in the past.
- A need to look at old problems and re-evaluate in order to determine new directions
- Haunted by the past
- Being stubborn and not making the necessary changes

SIX

QUALITIES

- A transition from one way of life to another
- This transition affects the whole family; symbolically represents changing to a new beginning where the outcome is unknown
- It could represent a divorce, someone leaving the home, a journey across water, a clearing of the way in order to discover what you want from love, home, and family
- Moving to a new residence

REVERSED

- Conflict in the home - a very difficult divorce; a separation from family that is painful
- Cancelled plans for a trip
- An unwanted move to a new residence

SEVEN

QUALITIES

- Landing in a new place
- Check your willingness to go on to the bigger picture, to move forward and actualize your scope of living from a larger standpoint
- Do not look back analyzing what has been done to get to this new position in life
- The tendency is to be paranoid and spend time analyzing the past rather than knowing you did the smart thing.
- Trusting and believing that the new direction can manifest to a new level
- Mental genius, sharpness of mind, quick wit with a tendency to double-check self by over-detailing, coupled with self-doubt, paranoia and hesitancy.

REVERSED

- Completely losing sight of a bigger view
- Stuck in over-analysis and details; rehashing every possible angle to the point of losing your reason for being.
- Not believing you are smart enough or that you have the tools for success
- Overly obsessive
- Stand back from a situation and ask, "Where am I letting the details get me down?"
- Tendency to self-sabotage by playing psychological warfare

EIGHT

QUALITIES

- Acknowledge what you have achieved
- Manifestation is all around, yet you cannot see it
- You are about to accomplish a new level of achievement in life
- The gate is opening to determine a new pathway of success
- Your vision is blinded to this because you've been looking only at what you didn't do with your life, rather than what you did.
- Sit down with paper and pen, and begin to review your life from a point of victory and accomplishment, rather than denial.

REVERSED

- Refusing to look at anything in life as a victory
- Spending a great deal of time wishing life could be different
- It is extremely important to rehash life from the positive rather than the negative - a need to cheer yourself on to victory
- Every night, before going to sleep, write down 5 accomplishments of the day. For example, getting the car washed, going to the grocery store, and picking up the dry cleaning. Acknowledge the little things on an ongoing daily basis and the subconscious mind will begin to see you as a winner!

NINE

QUALITIES

- Deeply entrenched in pain, depression, anxiety
- A need to go to bed and forget everyone around you
- Negative thoughts have become a reality
- No impetus to get out of bed and enjoy life
- Emotionally drained, depressed, anxious, exhausted; perhaps even a death wish card
- Could indicate sickness or someone getting ready to make a transition out of the physical
- Overly emotional, overly sensitive
- The way out of this card is to acknowledge what you have the most of and what you are the best at. Constantly reframe the thinking process towards the positive. Begin to talk to the Universe and ask for help. Know that it shall be granted by your acknowledgment of the positive.

REVERSED

- Extreme pain, depression, or anxiety
- Isolating, going inward
- Non-responsiveness
- Toxic - mentally, physically, and spiritually pulling in negativity

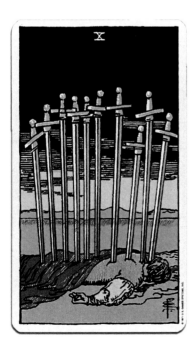

TEN

QUALITIES

- The pain of the past is now behind you - move forward into life
- The slate has been wiped clean.
- Pain is now history—you have moved beyond the negative thinking of others into redefining yourself with a brilliant new identity that takes you on a new course of power in the future

REVERSED

- Falling back into the pain of the past
- Unwilling to cut the apron strings with the negative aspects of life
- Feel most complete when giving away one's power
- A need to move on and leave the past and the pain in yesterday

PAGE of SWORDS.

PAGE

QUALITIES
- Embracing a new mental attitude
- Owning identity in a new way
- A teenager in the first stages of individuation and separation from dominance of his/her parents. Parents need to pat themselves on the back because the child's identity is strong enough to separate and individuate.

REVERSED
- Teenage rebellion is on the horizon.
- A need to cut the apron strings, yet parents are resisting the child's individuation which is making the rebellious search for identity a battle with authority.
- Begin to recognize and acknowledge the child as an individual rather than an extension of your ego—the battle will be less fatiguing.

KNIGHT of SWORDS.

KNIGHT

QUALITIES
- Mental reinforcement and encouragement is moving swiftly through your life allowing the space and courage to upgrade to a new level.

REVERSED
- A discouraging energy in the environment is holding you back, discouraging you, "popping your balloon", and not allowing your enthusiasm to motivate you.

QUEEN of SWORDS.

QUEEN

QUALITIES

- The logical woman
- A strong and determined woman with a penetrating mind who competes in a man's world by doing what men do
- Competitive
- Sharp mind, wit, and tongue
- Futuristic
- Intellectual
- Masculine polarity actualized in the woman-self
- Neat, organized, detailed, structured, penetrating, potent, dynamic—an adventurer and a risk-taker

REVERSED

- A cut-throat, two-faced woman who is judgmental, controlling, and stuck in her mental attitudes thus denying emotional expression
- Could be a back-stabber
- Compulsively detailed and structured
- Inflexible
- Lost in the masculine polarity
- A woman in denial of her feminine aspect
- Defensive, critical

KING of SWORDS.

KING

QUALITIES

- Male
- Great mental achiever
- An acknowledged authority in his field
- A man of great power and authority
- A scientist, inventor, computer whiz-bang, mathematician, architect, systems analyst, engineer
- Determined
- Conceptual—ability to actualize concepts
- Traditional, conventional
- Analytical—a good problem solver

REVERSED

- Controlling, stuck, stubborn, inflexible
- Does not see any options
- Critical, calculating man
- Cut-throat, two-faced, humorless, dry, defensive
- Destructively competitive
- No emotional expression
- No room for lateral thinking
- Tunnel vision
- Never received his own identity from his father
- Overly authoritative
- Insecure

PENTACLES
/COINS

Pentacles symbolize the Earth element and the Physical plane. The suit of Pentacles represents success. This is the Land of Results where concrete evidence of spiritual, mental, and emotional worlds manifests. This includes money, business, commerce, the body, health, home, car and, last but not least, self-worth and personal value. The results in your life are commensurate to the way you value yourself. Pentacles people are results-oriented, entrepreneurial, wealthy, abundant, and prosperous.

ACE

QUALITIES

- New beginnings in success and the material world
- A renewed sense of self-worth
- A new identity in success
- Prosperity and abundance
- A new investment that will "pay off" in a big way

REVERSED

- All that glitters is not gold
- Be careful of being fooled by something that looks good, but has no substance.
- Getting involved in a shady deal.

TWO

QUALITIES

- Time to balance the checkbook
- A favorable business decision
- Could be taking on a second job. In so doing, expect success.

REVERSED

- Not the time to make any decisions around money, business, or your material world—all options are not in yet.
- Listen to your heart, not your logic.
- Let go and gather more facts.

THREE

QUALITIES
- Good self-esteem and personal value around material success
- Ability to have fun and make money through your creative process
- It's time to take a commission for creative endeavors
- Have fun and go on a spending spree!

REVERSED
- The ego is tied up in the money you make and the way you make it
- You cannot see any possibilities around having fun and making money
- Spendthrift
- Poverty consciousness due to poor self-esteem and lack of self-worth
- Shopper's remorse

FOUR

QUALITIES
- A solid foundation for success
- Good business management
- Success in the world

REVERSED
- Money management required
- Need to follow or create a plan for success
- Not following the budget outline
- Re-evaluate your money/business management.

MINOR ARCANA-PENTACLES

FIVE

QUALITIES

- A change in prosperity consciousness is available to create expansion in money, business, and travel opportunities.
- Indicates positive changes – a physical move of residence, a change of revenue, a change in physical appearance.
- Business-related travel
- An opportunity to upgrade your social status.

REVERSED

- Unable to recognize the opportunity to change and expand
- Stuck in poverty consciousness
- Financial constrictions
- Blocked, stuck, unwilling to change
- Cancelled plans to move or take a trip due to lack of funds
- Financial forecast looks dim
- A financial setback

SIX

QUALITIES

- Practicing prosperity consciousness and being in harmony with the flow of abundance.
- A commitment to do a good job
- Earning money in the field of art, beauty, health, home. or service
- A time to tithe and spread the wealth
- Loving the way you make money and completely committed to it
- Knowing your self-worth and seeing/experiencing concrete evidence of it in the material world
- Complete satisfaction and commitment to work
- Could represent a real estate sale and getting the asking price

REVERSED

- Taking advantage of others in your business
- Material gain at the expense of others
- No satisfaction from doing the job, no self-value
- No level of commitment
- An uneven exchange for what you do and what you get back
- May be paying too much for a new home
- A need to redecorate the home, check health, and accent the beauty in life

SEVEN

QUALITIES

- A person with real financial know-how
- A financial wizard or genius
- Applying past experience to manifest financial success in the present
- Ability to create solutions around financial problems
- A time to step back and get a bigger picture of your financial forecast
- Time to acknowledge monetary dreams and what you want from success
- This card sets up the payoff.

REVERSED

- Repeating old, unsuccessful patterns around money and/or a financial picture
- Over-detailing and over-analyzing rather than expanding beyond the familiar area of learning.
- A tendency to focus on the "fly speck" instead of seeing the entire focus of what is being presented
- Constricted thinking
- Unnecessarily going back to the beginning and starting over again
- Unwilling to learn the lessons of success
- Over-analyzing money situations to the point of obsession, thus blocking any form of prosperity
- Lost vision of financial dreams and the bigger picture
- Shattered dreams of financial success
- Spinning your wheels

EIGHT

QUALITIES

- Manifestation of great wealth and abundance
- Getting the job and getting what you want out of it
- Concrete evidence of success manifested in physical form
- Goals achieved
- Making it happen - congratulate and acknowledge yourself
- Results of hard work now pay off
- Knowing what you want, going for it, and getting it.
- Good time to write a manifest list—do not leave anything out!

REVERSED

- The ability to get what you want is available, find out what it is
- It is imperative that you write a manifest list now. The money is there—call it in.
- Low self-worth holds back the flow of manifestation
- If you don't know what you want, cut out magazine pictures that attract you to bring in the awareness of what you want in life

NINE

QUALITIES
- The flow of abundance is so great that you are given the privilege to take your prosperity out into the world and make a contribution to the masses in whichever way you choose.
- This is the expansion of wealth into humanitarian endeavors.
- A patron of the arts
- Prosperity shifts into a larger format where the material world connects to a greater source
- Seeing and acknowledging abundance everywhere—in all aspects of life, on all levels of existence

REVERSED
- Unable to recognize the opportunity to change and expand
- Stuck in poverty consciousness
- Financial constrictions
- Blocked, stuck, unwilling to change
- Cancelled plans to move or take a trip due to lack of funds
- Financial forecast looks dim
- A financial setback

TEN

QUALITIES
- A new beginning in wealth and abundance that sets you up with an inheritance for future generations
- Abundance on all levels from having completed a project with perfection
- Money invested in the future that will pay off over time
- Could indicate an inheritance and/or a fortune—family money well invested for the future
- A new way of making money that sets the future up far beyond your wildest dreams
- A reinvestment of funds provides a new level of financial success.

REVERSED
- Unwilling to finish the job and bring it to completion
- Procrastinating on a project that needs to be completed
- Running a marathon and the finish line keeps extending beyond your grasp
- Fear of success or failure blocks completion

MINOR ARCANA-PENTACLES

PAGE of PENTACLES.

PAGE

QUALITIES
- Being open to new attitudes around success
- The beginning of a sense of personal value and positive self-esteem adds to the equation for success.
- Understanding self-worth on a new level
- A new job or new business in the beginning stages of development —could be a child's first job

REVERSED
- Thinking the world owes you a living
- Unwillingness to work for money
- Immature attitudes around money and success in business or career
- Could indicate a child with very low self-esteem; one who is lazy and unmotivated, who needs to experience success in the physical world by being paid on a task basis rather than given an allowance
- An irresponsible child

KNIGHT of PENTACLES.

KNIGHT

QUALITIES
- A new source of power that motivates and brings in a new level of success
- A person who brings in opportunities to make money in a career/business
- The perfect person to take your business out into the world on a new level
- A "go-for-it" salesperson
- A major motivating force behind your success

REVERSED
- Being held back from personal power and success
- Be careful and aware that someone could be ripping you off in business and/or your personal resources
- Not a good time to invest in any new endeavors in business
- Be careful of new investments, especially those brought to you through someone who looks like the picture of success
- Remember, all that glitters is not gold
- A con man
- Not a good time to take financial risks, personal or professional
- This could also be a gigolo

QUEEN of PENTACLES.

QUEEN

QUALITIES

- A natural woman, receptive to personal power and success
- Can mean a gift from an unexpected source
- Expect success when this card appears
- A proven authority in the material world
- A magnet for financial abundance. In touch with nature and all that is natural
- One who inherently knows how to get her needs met

REVERSED

- Spendthrift
- A victim around money
- Needy—Ignores physical reality through denial
- A gold digger
- Could indicate a financial loss
- A compulsive gambler or a charge-aholic
- Do not go into business with this woman. You will be taken advantage of and lose money.

KING of PENTACLES.

KING

QUALITIES

- Materiality at its best - Big Daddy Warbucks has arrived in all his glory!
- A great authority in business, finance, and success
- Generous
- Philanthropist
- Works well in marriage, or has an abundance of women in his life
- Expect success with this person
- Involvement with this person expands levels of awareness around manifestation in a full spectrum approach for living life to the fullest

REVERSED

- Unwilling to finish the job and bring it to completion
- Procrastinating on a project that needs to be completed
- Running a marathon and the finish line keeps extending beyond your grasp
- Fear of success or failure blocks completion

SYMBOLS

Symbols, the universal language of the Tarot, sidestep logic and go directly to the subconscious, freeing information hitherto locked in the cells, thus acting as the guide on an inner journey exploring resources available in the matrix of the collective unconscious and allowing for the expansion of consciousness.

Symbols are energy acquired in a space which defines the boundaries of awareness brought forward to pinpoint an area of conscious development in the moment. When working with symbols, energy is released; a moment of truth shifts into the body. You may giggle spontaneously, tears may come to your eyes, or your body might shiver. A sense of alignment may travel down your spine, making you stand tall for a moment. These are signs indicating prog-ress and movement that comes from the study of symbols.

This symbolic language is a dynamic tool for integration that synthesizes the union of universal truth into life. The Glossary of Symbols in this book is a beginning, a starting point, merely a springboard into the exploration of symbols and by no means a complete list. Symbols will speak to you in different ways at different times in your life. Let your own experience be your guide for defining symbols.

MAJOR ARCANA-SYMBOLS

HOW TO USE THE SYMBOLS SECTION

Each Tarot card is filled with a myriad of symbols. When reading your cards, a symbol may wave at you or spark your curiosity. Ask your intuition what it might mean to you and then back it up with the definitions provided in this section.

When first glancing at a Tarot card, notice which symbol stands out to you. It is a special message from the Tarot. You will also see how the symbols come alive in each card in different ways for each reading you do. The Symbols section of this book can help you understand and interpret these special messages about yourself.

The Symbols section is also a great tool to use after meditating on a card. When you open your eyes upon ending your meditation the subconscious modality is still at work. You might notice the lantern of The Hermit glowing, the fragrance of roses may come over you while viewing The Magician card, or the wheel might be spinning on The Wheel of Fortune.

MAJOR ARCANA SYMBOLS

The following section provides the meaning of the many symbols found on the Major Arcana cards. Flip to the appropriate card to learn about its symbols.

MAJOR ARCANA SYMBOLS–THE FOOL

STICK: A symbol of measurement indicating good self-esteem. Self-esteem is required for risk-taking.

FEATHER/PLUME: The feather of the Phoenix, a symbol of rebirth

WHITE SUN: Symbol of source, prior to life, not of our solar system , indicates that the setting of this card is not here on Earth, but on the other side, before Life.

9 PINWHEELS: 9 pinwheels of consciousness, indicating completion of other lifetimes - awareness from past experiences already completed

KNAPSACK: Baggage from past lives – karma

FLAME ON SHIRT: Symbol of eternal light

WHITE ROSE: Symbolizes our connection to Spirit

ORANGE SLEEVES: Ready for the world, impulsive

YELLOW SKY: Indicates pure intention coming from a light source— solar energy

WHITE UNDERSHIRT: Purity and innocence

GREEN TUNIC: Natural expression

MOUNTAIN PEAKS: Frozen consciousness, waiting in storage to be used for the new life, the height of awareness, the ten peak experiences to be experienced through life – The Fool risks reason for a mountaintop experience. (The same peaks are shown on Hermit (IX) and Judgement (XX) cards.)

GREEN LEGGINGS: Natural understanding

YELLOW BOOTS: Foundation and footing in the light and logic

THE FOOL.

YOUTH: Open arms ready to embrace all of life, symbolizes the promise of new things to come, a new generation bringing in new awareness and potential into life, a phasing in of new attitudes, adding the next equation to experience, open and totally available, looking up, indicating faith in all that is to come—optimism

LOWER MOUNTAINS: One is the mountain of isolation and loneliness. The other is the mountain of wisdom. Together they indicate perseverance to continue to grow and achieve. The valley in between is the road of balance/integration.

DOG: Symbol of unconditional love, man's best friend, primal instincts, our connection to nature

CLIFF: Referred to as "the seat of reason", a symbol of risking, going beyond reason, being on the edge. Indicates the instant before risk, the moment that expands beyond logic.

ROD: *(Twin flames) Inner and outer forces working the axiom, "as above, so below", the dualistic approach to life includes both ends of the spectrum, his hand is holding the center of the rod indicating that the center (between "above" and "below") is where manifestation occurs.*

BACKGROUND: *Comes from solar power (masculine), attention and focus, converts foreground from a state of pure light*

INFINITY: *Life eternal, as above, so below, shows us our linear and spatial awareness, ethereal and material connection, a sideways "8", the number of manifestation.*

WHITE ROBE: *Purity of intention*

CUP: *Emotional - tool for creative fulfillment.*

RED ROBE: *Connection to passion for and action in life*

HAND: *Pointing with index finger (the Will), here and now is where power converts, you start from where you stand in the moment, manifestation is NOW!*

PENTACLE: *Physical - tool for results and manifestation*

WAND: *Spiritual - tool for inspiration and growth.*

SNAKE BELT: *All forms of truth feed on themselves – symbol for the continuum*

SWORD: *Mental - tool for progress and individuation.*

HIEROGLYPHICS: *Indication of boundaries*

THE MAGICIAN.

TABLE: *The table of life, the working level, the center, all tools (talents) of life are displayed out front and above board.*

TOOLS: *The tools for life to be used and integrated on the four planes of awareness; spiritual, emotional, mental, and physical.*

LEFT PILLAR: *The feminine principle – Receptivity, Doorway to the inner world expands beyond logic.*

PILLARS: *The polarity principles: positive/negative, male/female, marks the spot where initiation occurs, the point where outer world and inner world meet and the mystery of life connects – conscious and unconscious awareness*

RIGHT PILLAR: *The masculine principle – Positive - Doorway to the outer world.*

OLIVE BRANCHES: *Vitality of life*

HEADDRESS: *3 phases of the moon: New Moon- (waxing), Bringing in. Full Moon-Manifestation. Old Moon-(waning), letting go. Symbolizes cyclical time, the feminine connection to the moon time/night time, subconscious, light in the dark, receptivity, reflection, and space.*

PALMS: *Victory of life*

POMEGRANATES: *Fertility, the seed of life*

CROSS: *Integration of masculine (logic) and feminine (intuition)*

THE HIGH PRIESTESS.

VEIL: *Tapestry of Life. Separating conscious and subconscious, the known and unknown, duality awareness, material/ethereal.*

BLUE ROBE: *Color of the subconscious, the Soul and emotion – Femininity flows, thus creating the stream of consciousness which flows throughout the Tarot.*

BLUE BACKGROUND: *The depth of your Soul, the subconscious connection to the mystery of life, the conduit, intuition, the Tapestry of Life before Life.*

SCROLL: *The Book of Knowledge*

CRESCENT MOON: *Symbolizes receptivity, magnetic forces at work, feminine understanding*

GREY CUBIC STONE: *The midpoint between black and white equals grey; the color of wisdom.*

YELLOW GROUND: *The point where logic meets intuition (masculine meets feminine), adding movement to consciousness, the conductor (water) adds movement to consciousness, the light of the sun meets the lunar influence.*

12 STARS: *(above wreath) In touch with her heavenly nature, 12 signs of the Zodiac, 12 tribes of Israel*

SCEPTER: *This short scepter is a symbol of ruling in areas of closeness.*

BACKGROUND: *A natural setting indicating the connection to nature and the external product of love and nurturing.*

CROWN: *Symbol of victory*

NECKLACE: *7 Pearls – Nature's symbol of wisdom*

POMEGRANATES: *(on gown) Indicates fertility, willingness to love and integrate*

PREGNANCY: *Pregnant with fife, fulfilled through her fertility process*

ANKHS: *behind Pillow: Represent integrated receptivity*

STREAM: *The stream of consciousness continues and drops down a level from The High Priestess (II) to the Earth plane.*

CUSHIONS: *on Throne: Indicates comfort with the natural, passionate self – The color red indicates that the seat of passion is The Empress' power.*

III

THE EMPRESS.

GREY STONE: *Integration (black & white = grey) of passion, covered with red pillows.*

ANKH: *Symbol of Venus; the Feminine, the integration of masculine and feminine principles, positive (penetrative) and negative (receptive).*

SHIELD: *Heart – Symbol of love.*

WHEAT: *Symbol of nurturing and abundance – the staff of Life*

CROWN: *Authority*

BACKGROUND: *Orange, Structure*

BEARD: *Wisdom*

SCEPTER: *Symbol of government*

RED SCARF: *Symbolizes action and the ability to take action in the world*

STREAM: *Stream of consciousness flows behind him, inner awareness is available to him at any time as a resource*

RAM'S HEAD *on Shoulder: Courage to face the future*

MOUNTAIN RANGES: *Perseverance, sits between 2 mountain ranges of wisdom and understanding, past history is successful (mountains are in the background)*

RAMS HEADS: *Sign of Aries; the opening forces of Life, sheer power, indicates breakthroughs on all 4 levels – the power of the head: mental/masculine; in all areas, in all angles.*

GREY THRONE: *Sits in the Power of Wisdom; an integrated man of the world*

ARMOR: *Protection*

MAJOR ARCANA SYMBOLS–THE HIEROPHANT

HEBREW LETTER: *Shin = Tooth. To change, repeat, the interchange of consciousness between body, mind, and spirit in search of illumination.*

EAR FLAPS: *Conveys inner hearing, the importance of interpretation.*

WHITE SLEEVES: *Purity of intention*

7 FOLDS IN ROBE: *7 chakras*

YELLOW "Y": *Reaching out to expand and integrate higher knowledge into life.*

TRIPLE TIARA: *Sovereignty over spirit, mind, and body.*

BACKGROUND: *Gray, Integration*

BLUE UNDERGARMENT: *Symbol of mercy*

RED ROBE: *Symbol of might*

WHITE YOKE with *Strip: Principle of extremities – line down middle is the midline of balance. 3 crosses and the diamond on the strip of yoke represent integration of spirit, mind, and body into the world.*

BLACK & WHITE STRIPS: *Guidelines for the path of wisdom – integration of black and white, good/bad, right/wrong*

CROSSED KEYS: *Unlock the cosmic secrets of the inner and outer worlds – the keys to knowledge.*

2 FIGURES: *Two Initiates: One wears a robe of roses indicating the path of passion. One wears a robe of lilies indicating the path of purity. Both paths lead to wisdom and understanding.*

58

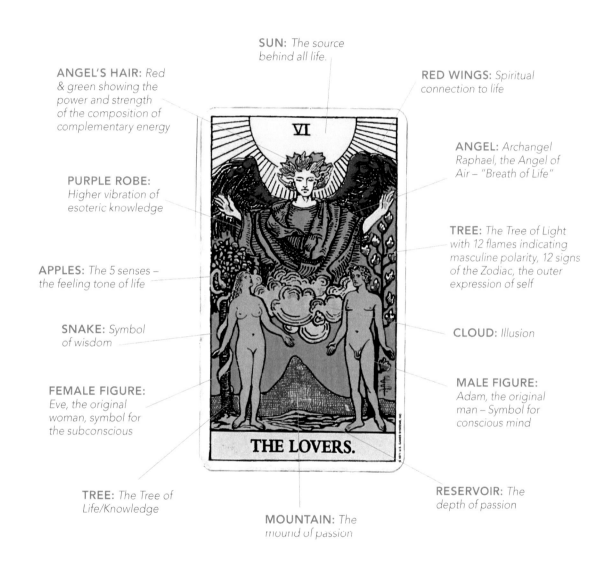

SUN: *The source behind all life.*

ANGEL'S HAIR: *Red & green showing the power and strength of the composition of complementary energy*

RED WINGS: *Spiritual connection to life*

ANGEL: *Archangel Raphael, the Angel of Air – "Breath of Life"*

PURPLE ROBE: *Higher vibration of esoteric knowledge*

TREE: *The Tree of Light with 12 flames indicating masculine polarity, 12 signs of the Zodiac, the outer expression of self*

APPLES: *The 5 senses – the feeling tone of life*

SNAKE: *Symbol of wisdom*

CLOUD: *Illusion*

FEMALE FIGURE: *Eve, the original woman, symbol for the subconscious*

MALE FIGURE: *Adam, the original man – Symbol for conscious mind*

TREE: *The Tree of Life/Knowledge*

MOUNTAIN: *The mound of passion*

RESERVOIR: *The depth of passion*

CROWN: *8-pointed star says authority and direction projected through insights*

4 PILLARS: *The pillars of reason and logic. North, East, South, and West, indicates Earth plane, the 4 worlds: spiritual, mental, emotional, and physical*

CANOPY OF STARS: *Universal consciousness connected to the world of reason (the chariot).*

LAUREL WREATH: *Accomplishment and victory in the outer world*

CHARIOTEER: *Masculine power, outer personality to be used in outer world experience*

BREAST PLATE: *Logic over feelings, mind over matter*

STAFF: *Symbol for will and intention that drives man through life*

WAXING & WANING MOONS: *(on shoulders) Intuition integrated in his worldly appearance, feminine awareness, symbol for Cancer (inner work).*

ARMOR: *Protection needed while traveling through time and life*

BELT & HIEROGLYPH: *Map of consciousness*

CUFF PLATES: *Conveys the defensive nature of protection, self-defense*

CITIES: *Inner mind manifesting in the outer world*

WALL: *Defined area of projected thought (the mind), boundaries and limitation*

WHEELS: *Broad-based, indicating broad sweeping changes and movement*

RIVER: *Stream of consciousness flowing (inner self), depth of feeling*

SPHINXES: *Symbol of curiosity – Motivation to obtain answers*

BLACK SPHINX: *inner world*

WHITE SPHINX: *outer world*

WINGED DISK: *The power of will and purpose in the mind to soar towards awareness and victory*

SHIELD: *Protection*

ROTA: *Like a top or gyroscope shows us movement in the outer & inner plane of awareness, a symbol of balance, an auto-pilot*

CUBE: *The sound construction of logic here on the Earth plane, the grounded reality we stand in while living.*

INFINITY SIGN: *Blending consciousness (the Universe) and nature, back to The Magician card, "as above, so below"*

YELLOW BACKGROUND: *Solar energy – Outer self-expression*

CROWN OF ROSES: *The crown of nature – authority is obtained from natural awareness and the expression of desire*

WOMAN: *Symbol of the subconscious – shows us that the primal (natural) expression comes through the woman-self*

WHITE DRESS: *The purity of nature and its intention to blend with consciousness to promote evolution*

BELT OF ROSES: *Shows us our connection to the natural and primal passion of life*

HAND: *On Lion's Mouth: Indicates the need to communicate naturally*

LION: *Symbol of our primal, natural self, source of life force, the passion of life, the king of the beasts, shows us the authority of nature within, when you give your natural self-power, more of life becomes available to you.*

MOUNTAIN: *Perseverance – through perseverance comes strength*

LANDSCAPE: *Natural setting indicating this card is about the physical process, man's connection to nature, the integration of life force*

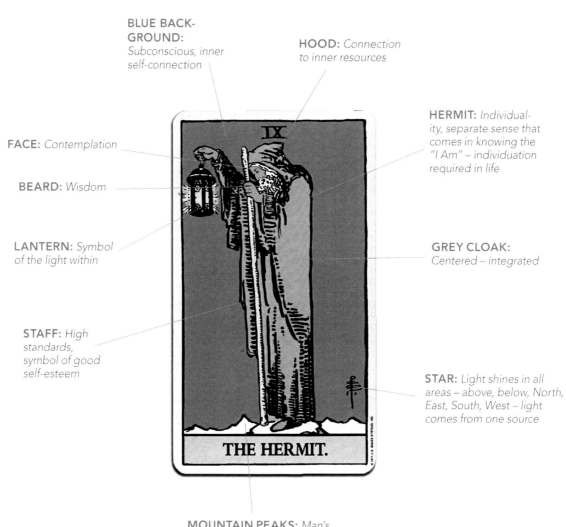

BLUE BACK-GROUND: *Subconscious, inner self-connection*

HOOD: *Connection to inner resources*

FACE: *Contemplation*

HERMIT: *Individuality, separate sense that comes in knowing the "I Am" – individuation required in life*

BEARD: *Wisdom*

LANTERN: *Symbol of the light within*

GREY CLOAK: *Centered – integrated*

STAFF: *High standards, symbol of good self-esteem*

STAR: *Light shines in all areas – above, below, North, East, South, West – light comes from one source*

THE HERMIT.

MOUNTAIN PEAKS: *Man's need to climb to the height of his awareness, the isolated experience that comes with individuality, man's need to go back to source and reconnect, peak experience*

MAJOR ARCANA SYMBOLS—WHEEL OF FORTUNE

CLOUDS: *Illusion, consciousness about to change, indicates the climate or atmosphere of any given situation*

SPHINX: *Curiosity, movement, stages of development, blue represents the subconscious*

BLUE BACKGROUND: *Ether*

ALCHEMY SYMBOLS: *(center of wheel), Represents exchange and interplay of energy, thus generating movement.*

SWORD: *Double edges of the mind, thus integrates the subconscious of the sphinx with mental awareness*

BOOKS: *Acquisition and application of knowledge available in each area of development*

HEBREW LETTERS: *Yod, Heh, Vav, Hed. Jehovah, Yahweh. Aramaic equivalent – I, H, V, H*

RED JACKAL: *Hermanubis (half Hermes, half Anubis); two gods of Egypt mixed in one form. Hermes – outer self, communication and expression. Anubis —Inner awareness. Red is the color of action, passion, and desire*

SERPENT: *Kundalini energy, life force moving inward, yellow indicates light, solar energy, going within, 10 waves in serpent show us the 10 steps in life*

FOUR CORNERS: *Upper Left: Human, Aquarius, Air, Mental plane Lower Left: Bull, Taurus, Earth, Physical plane Lower Right: Lion, Leo, Fire, Spiritual plane Upper Right: Eagle, Scorpio, Water, Emotional plane*

CENTER WHEEL: *The compass of consciousness, evolution and involution, motivation and time to promote direction (outer) in cycles to promote development (inner). TORA: (letters counterclockwise) Knowledge and law. TAROT: (letters clockwise) Road of life, external motivation and direction, evolution. ROTA: Internal motivation, involution. ORAT: "To speak your truth."*

MAJOR ARCANA SYMBOLS–JUSTICE

VIOLET VEIL: *Mystery and hidden information, dualistic approach to right and wrong, obscuring the truth*

YELLOW BACKGROUND: *Source of light*

SQUARE ON CROWN: *Logical foundation for the structure of justice*

GREY PILLARS: *Mark the place in the centered experience where known and unknown realities meet and become a whole expression*

SWORD: *Double-edged quality of the mind showing us the split in awareness that makes both sides of any given situation available to us in evaluating balance*

CROWN: *Symbol of authority, positive and negative squares showing that the goal of authority is to keep all energies even and balanced in linear and spatial awareness*

GREEN CAPE: *Simplicity of nature and its automatic system of checks and balances*

SCALES: *Perfect balance, trust that everything that happens will eventually have to reconcile itself to balance, all energies get corrected here*

CIRCLE: *Inner and outer equalization*

GREY THRONE: *The seat of power is integration.*

RED ROBE: *Expression of life's action and reaction*

BLUE UNDERGARMENT: *Inner knowing – intuition*

GREY BACKGROUND: *Integration*

YELLOW SLIPPERS: *Soul's connection to source*

LEGS: *Positioned in a reverse "4", the number that relates to the world of logic, the 4 is reversed showing him "hanging out," contrary to the world and logic, the position shows taking "time out" from the world, thus defying logic.*

T-CROSS: *The Tree of Life, cosmic connection to life, integration of physical and spiritual awareness*

RED LEGGINGS: *Action, Mars, Physical, Passion – tied to the Tree of Life indicating time out*

LEAVES: *Physical and spiritual growth*

FOOT: *Soul's attachment to Heaven, spiritual understanding*

BLUE JACKET: *Subconscious connection. Time to relate to the void and be receptive – Color of passive-receptive subconscious*

YELLOW HALO: *Enlightenment – awareness comes in the moment when we get ourselves out of the way*

HAIR: *Strength, acceptance, detachment*

STAFF: *Measure of cycles and time, evolutionary cycles involved in changing and completing patterns in Life and Death, regeneration*

WHITE ROSE: *White rose of spirit, void of life force, 10 petals indicate completion*

PLUME: *Wilted Phoenix feather indicates that release is instrumental in rebirth – the red color symbolizes life's connection to death.*

BANNER: *Life's connection to Death is always in the space of time*

SUN: *Rising or setting*

SKULL MASK: *Symbol of the unknown factor or fear associated with death, change, or transformation – we know change is inevitable, but we don't know when it's coming.*

CITY: *Existence on the other side, a confirmation of life after death*

MAN: *In Black Armor, expresses the need to be receptive to death/ change*

TOWERS: *Marks the door of departure where transformation occurs*

BOAT: *Life flows eternal in consciousness*

WHITE HORSE: *Symbol of change moving toward you – power comes through changes*

RIVER: *Flows in the background – stream of consciousness is still flowing symbolizing that death is a physical phenomenon – shows us the continuum of consciousness.*

GREY BACKGROUND: *Integration*

FOREGROUND: *Battlefield with people of all ages and walks of life – Shows us that the battleground for life and death is a common denominator for all humanity*

RAYS: *Radiant light that comes with purpose and intention*

GREY BACKGROUND: *Integration*

BLONDE HAIR: *Connection of light source to the mind*

YELLOW HALO: *Enlightenment, awareness comes in the moment when we get ourselves out of the way*

WINGS: *Knowledge coming from a higher vibration*

HEBREW LETTERS: *Yod, Heh, Vav, Heh, Jehovah. Corresponds to The Wheel of Fortune (X)*

SOLAR DISK: *Symbol of inner vision, reflection and protection*

ANGEL: *Archangel Michael, Angel of Fire*

TRIANGLE: *Balance of power, external and internal forces at work*

WHITE GOWN: *Purity*

2 URNS: *One masculine, one feminine, past and future, the context that holds life. Gold color is an indication of light source or outer self-connection.*

SUNRISE/SUNSET: *Beginning or ending of a process*

7 DOTS: *The 7 inner lights of man, chakra system*

IRISES: *The mythological Goddess of the Rainbow, the symbol of Promise – Iris was in charge of assisting crossing souls who have trouble letting go by cutting their cords, thus releasing their souls from their bodies.*

MOUNTAINS: *Peak experiences*

PATH: *The Path of Life leading to the mountains, passing between them, indicating that the middle path of moderation (the way of the Buddha) is the easiest path to take.*

WATER: *Blending of consciousness and content, mixing and experimenting, trial and error, discriminating, flowing through all levels: spiritual, emotional, mental, and physical, water (intuition and the subconscious) flowing from the left urn (feminine, inner, subconscious) into the right urn (male, outer, consciousness).*

FEET: *One on land, one in water, spiritual and physical understanding at work and in balance*

MAJOR ARCANA SYMBOLS–THE DEVIL

BLACK BACKGROUND: *Receptivity, the polarity of light, the absence of light, darkness, void*

REVERSED PENTAGRAM: *Downfall – misplaced energy, "taking a nose dive", living life from the root chakra, reversal, polarity*

HORNS: *Symbol of Capricorn*

GOAT FACE: *Indicates stubbornness – inflexibility*

RAISED HAND: *Symbol of Saturn etched in the palm, the planet that limits in order to learn – Friction and inertia promote growth*

BEARD: *Indicates that he has been around a long time, promoting learning lessons to be experienced for man*

BAT WINGS: *Bats fly in the dark, symbol for the Angel of Darkness (Lucifer)*

LOWER BODY: *The bottom half of an eagle, lower forms of Scorpio, sexuality based in sensation alone*

BROWN BODY: *Struggle in physical reality – absence of spirituality*

WOMAN: *Subconscious mind*

TORCH FLAMES: *Casts no light, expression of passion void of connection to Spirit*

FRUIT: *Appetite for lust , symbol of intoxication*

THE DEVIL.

FLAMES: *Ignited desire driven by lust*

MAN: *Conscious mind*

HALF-CUBE: *Materiality, absence of spirituality, Shows one side of reality, the picture is not whole, "What you see is what you get."*

CHAINS: *Limitation, lack of freedom, stuck to blocks, connection to the material world – Though the chains are perceived as binding, they are, in reality, easily removed.*

TOWER: *False pretenses, above-it-all attitude, isolation, higher than mighty, narrow-mindedness, separateness*

BLACK BACKGROUND: *Void, empty, receptivity, absence of light*

LIGHTNING BOLT: *Help from a higher source*

3 WINDOWS: *Holier-than-thou, above-it-all vision, belonging to the ego*

FIRE: *Purification and elimination*

12 FLAMES: *(left side of tower), 12 tribes of Israel – story of the Tower of Babel, the dissemination of people in different forms of expression*

10 FLAMES: *(right Side of Tower), Enlightened new beginnings*

CLOUDS: *Illusion, change in consciousness about to occur*

FALLING FIGURES: *Man (conscious mind) and woman (subconscious mind) landing head first to knock sense into them, the breaking away of thinking patterns that are no longer appropriate.*

CROWN: *False authority.*

CLOTHES: *Red and blue, colors of passion and compassion*

THE TOWER.

GROUND: *False foundation, not grounded in reality, lacking a solid base*

STAR: *8 points, manifestation of opportunities, stellar performance, hope, direction, navigation, being on course, guidance, connection to unknown galaxies, insights, motivation, inspiration*

7 SMALL STARS: *7 chakras, inner lights of man, inner self-connection to cosmos, insight, meditation*

BLUE BACKGROUND: *Cosmic consciousness*

BIRD: *Sacred Ibis, Egyptian bird known for its ability to fish, symbolizes transformation of consciousness*

WOMAN: *Subconscious connection to nature and evolution, change comes through the woman-self, nakedness, open to opportunity, free, exposed – vulnerable, natural*

BUSH: *Opportunity to grow and branch out in new direction*

MOUNTAINS: *Man's willingness to continue to climb to new heights*

FLOWERS: *The inner beauty of life, Spirit's manifestation in the physical, passion taking root*

URNS: *Vessels for transformation*

FOOT ON WATER: *The delicate balance of consciousness*

5 RIVULETS OF WATER: *Adding new awareness to the five senses*

POURING: *Transforming consciousness, manifesting it on Earth, and simultaneously adding to the collective consciousness*

KNEE ON EARTH: *Balance applied on the Physical plane*

RINGS: *(in water) Symbol of inner development, mediation*

POOL: *Area of collected consciousness made available for us to dip into at any time.*

BLUE BACKGROUND: *Nighttime, shadow side, dream state, obscurity, subconscious*

MOON: *Reflection, femininity, intuition, cycles, light in the dark*

ECLIPSE: *The light (sun) is in back of the moon showing us that enlightenment comes after we have faced ourselves in the dark, symbolizes hidden information and mystery leading us to the light*

TOWERS: *Man's need for protection, marks the spot where altered states of awareness begin. Intuitive arts, meditation, and dream work take place here.*

WINDOWS: *Symbolize inner vision, non-physical entry, astral travel or out-of-body experiences*

MOUNTAIN PEAKS: *Peak experience, higher self-manifestation*

DOG: *Tamed version of animal kingdom, symbol of evolution, man's connection to animal, man's best friend barking at the moon, warning man to stay on the path.*

RAIN SHOWER: *Consists of 15 Yods equaling the number 6, a Yod symbolizes the "I AM", man's individuality reigns supreme, thus providing an exchange of energy promoting evolution towards the light or enlightenment, a change of consciousness occurs when evolving through the dark side of self to re-identify itself on a new level.*

WOLF: *Primal instincts, represents animal kingdom, the untamed side of self*

FIELD: *Area of learning, field of awareness on the path of life, potential for expansion and exploration off the path, thus making the path windy rather than straight.*

CRAYFISH: *Symbol of evolution*

POOL: *A collected area of consciousness, birthing place from which all life evolves and exploration off the path, thus making the path windy rather than straight.*

YELLOW PATH: *The pathway to the light, indicates others have traveled before you*

STONES: *Representation of the mineral kingdom*

BLUE BACKGROUND: *Consciousness meets up with the light*

FACE: *The outer expression of self*

WAVY RAYS: *Light integrated in 4 worlds; spiritual, mental, emotional, and physical*

SUN: *Solar power, source of life, radiance, warmth, enlightenment, expression of our outer self, our personality shining brightly for all to see and experience. Consistency born new every day, individuality re-expressing itself every day, thus giving life.*

4 SUNFLOWERS: *Growth of enlightenment in four worlds; spiritual, mental, emotional, and physical.*

PLUME: *Phoenix feather symbolizes rebirth.*

WREATH: *Light's connection to life in six directions: North, East, South, West, above, and below*

NAKED CHILD: *Rebirth, having nothing to hide, embracing life from a totally open space*

RAYS: *Straight rays – Straight projection of self*

BANNER: *The passionate connection to life in all areas of awareness*

4 WAVES: *Enlightenment integrated in the four worlds: spiritual, mental, emotional, and physical*

WALL: *The blocks are now behind, boundaries and limitations defined, breakthrough*

HORSE: *Symbol of power, horsepower, motivation, movement*

ANGEL: *Archangel Gabriel, the Angel of Water, higher source realization, elevation to the next step of development*

BLUE BACKGROUND: *Consciousness*

TRUMPET: *Symbol of sound, the first step of manifestation, calling in a higher frequency, a blast of energy, thus generating movement, awakening, a calling, tuning the vibration of the Soul*

CLOUDS: *A change of consciousness*

BANNER: *Displays the cross of St. George, integration in four areas, production, connection to life*

7 SOUND WAVES: *(from Trumpet),Tuning of the chakras*

MOUNTAIN PEAKS: *Peak experience, higher self-manifestation*

WATER: *Reservoir of knowledge now complete*

GREY FIGURES: *(Background). Reflection of consciousness, the need to look at self, what has been produced here and in other areas simultaneously and synergistically*

GREY FIGURES: *(Foreground). The integrated woman-self/man-self, child is the product of integration*

COFFINS: *Symbol of completion in the Third dimension (physical form), opening to a new level, the Fourth dimension*

BLUE BACKGROUND: *Universal completion – sky power*

PURPLE SCARF: *Blending life (red) with consciousness (blue) making purple, the color of esoteric knowledge integrated on 4 levels (spiritual, mental, emotional, and physical) indicated by the four bends in the scarf.*

CREATURES: *4 worlds, 4 seasons, 4 directions; outer self-completion in all areas. Delineation of time, cycles, and seasons. Upper Left: Human, Aquarius, Air, Mental plane. Lower Left: Bull, Taurus, Earth, Physical plane. Lower Right: Lion, Leo, Fire, Spiritual plane. Upper Right: Eagle, Scorpio, Water, Emotional plane*

DANCER: *Mastery on the Physical plane*

2 BATONS: *Magician's twin-flamed wands, one in each hand, indicating eternal light mastered within and without,- as above, so below.*

GARLAND: *Victory, success, prosperity, happiness, attainment, the "O" of opportunity*

CLOUDS: *Illusion or consciousness, determined by the point of view*

RED BANDS: *The infinity symbol in red circling around the wreath showing that The Magician's intention has now been completed. As above, so below is realized here.*

notes

minor arcana-symbols

The following section provides the meaning of the many symbols found on the Minor Arcana cards. Flip to the appropriate card to learn about its symbols.

PERSONALITY CARDS

Personality cards describe the personalities of people who characterize the qualities of their suit.

- Wands people are inspirational, growth-oriented, charismatic, fiery, and explosive.

- Cups people are emotional, creative, loving, and receptive.

- Swords people are mental, logical, analytical, and organized.

- Pentacles people are results-oriented, entrepreneurial, wealthy, abundant, and prosperous.

We all meet people who teach, motivate and challenge us. Remember, the Tarot means, "Road to Life." The personality cards take on the characteristics of the people we encounter who promote our growth and development. Each suit has a "family" of people who express characteristics of expertise and awareness in their defined areas.

Each family has four members: a Page, a Knight, a Queen and a King. Pages represent a younger person (anyone younger than you). Knights are the motivating force in the family; people who move you to the next level. Queens represent women in your life who reflect your feelings. They describe your receptive qualities and emotional concerns. Kings represent the men in your life who reflect your logical, thinking, and the way you take action in your life.

WANDS

Wands symbolize the Fire element. They indicate the Spiritual plane, which provides enlightenment, inspiration, progress, and growth. Wands promote the ability to be inspired and go for greater glory. Wands also indicate career progress and growth.

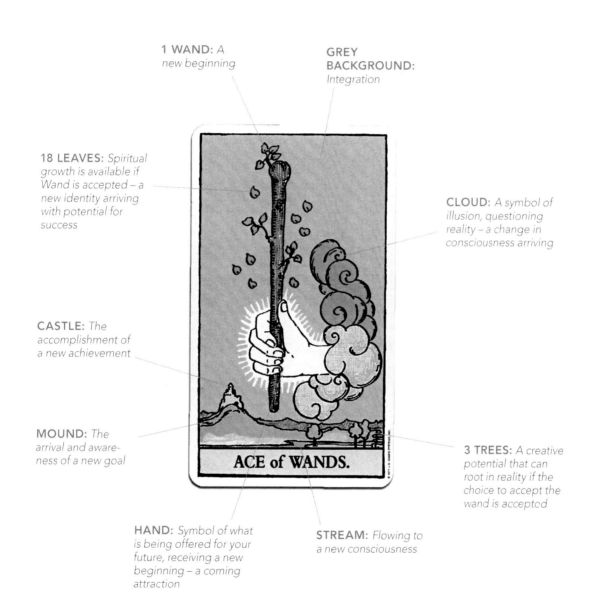

1 WAND: *A new beginning*

GREY BACKGROUND: *Integration*

18 LEAVES: *Spiritual growth is available if Wand is accepted – a new identity arriving with potential for success*

CLOUD: *A symbol of illusion, questioning reality – a change in consciousness arriving*

CASTLE: *The accomplishment of a new achievement*

MOUND: *The arrival and aware-ness of a new goal*

3 TREES: *A creative potential that can root in reality if the choice to accept the wand is accepted*

HAND: *Symbol of what is being offered for your future, receiving a new beginning – a coming attraction*

STREAM: *Flowing to a new consciousness*

MINOR ARCANA SYMBOLS—WANDS

GREY BACKGROUND: *The atmosphere is motivated by wisdom and the ability to be open to new light, awareness.*

2 WANDS: *Doubling your success by accepting the new potential offered with the Ace of Wands – the two wands are about accepting the expansion in life rather than vacillating.*

MAN: *Wearing Red – A symbol of success that comes from action (passion)*

GLOBE: *Indicates success in the world – when we double our opportunities we can hold the world in the palm of our hand*

MOUNTAIN RANGE: *A range of goals accomplished in the physical dimension*

RIGHT HAND: *A symbol of success realized*

LEFT HAND: *A symbol of accepting opportunity – receiving power is operating*

OCEAN: *Consciousness is manifesting through awareness –The Spiritual connection is realized*

VERANDA: *A sign of an increased and expanded view in life that comes when one accepts new opportunity*

FAMILY CREST: *Family crest with crossed red roses & white lilies shows the merging of two pathways, doubles the opportunities for success.*

THE VIEW: *Widening your horizon for success*

YELLOW BACKGROUND: *A sign that good times are here when we use our creative potential*

LEFT WAND: *The arrival of a new opportunity.*

MAN: *Red, a symbol of success that comes from action (passion). Green activates the realization that abundance is on its way.*

YELLOW OCEAN: *Indicates that a focused intention, combined with consciousness, is necessary for manifestation.*

3 WANDS: *Being ignited through the power of creativity*

RIGHT WAND: *Manifesting potential is realized.*

THREE SHIPS: *Manifestation is on its way. "His ships are coming in!"*

GREEN & ORANGE LANDSCAPE: *His grounded reality is creativity (orange) that brings abundance (green).*

STANDING ON A CLIFF: *A symbol of a bigger view brings more for the future.*

YELLOW BACKGROUND: *A sign of good times. Happy Days are here!*

CANOPY OF ROSES: *A celebration of marriage – Celebrating a ritual for setting up a grounded spiritual reality.*

4 WANDS: *Foundation for a happy, successful life.*

CASTLE: *A major goal accomplished*

MAN: *Wearing blue. Indicates that he is open to his feelings. Roses – He is open to celebration through his passion.*

WOMAN: *Wearing red. Indicates that she is open to her passion. Lilies – She is open to celebrate her purity*

YELLOW FOREGROUND: *The foundation is set up with a happy, enlightened structure.*

BLUE BACKGROUND:
A sign of a change in the atmosphere motivated by consciousness.

5 YOUNG MEN:
Indicates new thought on the move. New ideas presenting a different way to experience life.

5 WANDS:
Action, change, expansion, variety

MULTI-COLORED GROUND:
The foundation is set up for variety.

BLUE BACKGROUND: *The atmosphere is motivated by consciousness awareness.*

WAND & OLIVE WREATH: *Symbol of the vitality and stamina it takes to make a change and be victorious.*

6 WANDS: *Victory*

LAUREL WREATH: *A symbol of advancement in leadership.*

MAN: *Wearing Red – Action leads to victory.*

GROUP OF MEN: *(in background each carrying a wand) Unity of conscious alignment*

WHITE HORSE: *A symbol of power, the ability to take action – white represents purification and change.*

GREEN BLANKET: *Riding toward abundance, service, and love.*

MINOR ARCANA SYMBOLS–WANDS

BLUE BACKGROUND: *The atmosphere is motivated by consciousness awareness.*

MAN: *Wearing Green and Yellow. Being ready to take on a new level of growth motivated by the light.*

7 WANDS: *Big thinking and adding a new dimension*

ORANGE SHOES: *A sign of understanding creative power.*

STREAM: *A flow of new consciousness is being planted on the earth.*

GREEN LANDSCAPE: *The foundation is set up with growth in mind.*

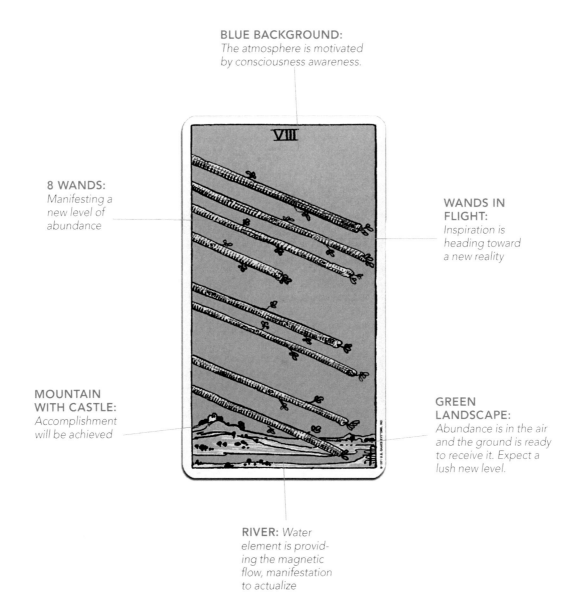

BLUE BACKGROUND:
The atmosphere is motivated by consciousness awareness.

8 WANDS:
Manifesting a new level of abundance

WANDS IN FLIGHT:
Inspiration is heading toward a new reality

MOUNTAIN WITH CASTLE:
Accomplishment will be achieved

GREEN LANDSCAPE:
Abundance is in the air and the ground is ready to receive it. Expect a lush new level.

RIVER: *Water element is providing the magnetic flow, manifestation to actualize*

BLUE BACKGROUND:
The atmosphere is motivated by consciousness awareness.

9 WANDS:
See the cycle completed

WHITE BANDAGE:
Shows that his thinking is no longer interfering with his ability to be fulfilled.

MAN: *(wearing orange & white) Creative power has been purified and completion will soon become fulfillment.*

8 WANDS:
(background) Acknowledgement is now necessary to complete the cycle of spiritual advancement.

GREEN MOUNTAINS:
Goals have been manifested to the heights of one's awareness.

GREY FOREGROUND:
His foundation is integrated masculine/feminine, Spirit/ Earth, feelings/thinking. He is standing on wisdom.

BLUE BACKGROUND:
The atmosphere is motivated by consciousness awareness.

10 WANDS:
Setting up a formula for a new beginning

FINISH LINE:
Completion, one step away from the new beginning.

VILLAGE & TREES:
New life and new growth coming his way.

ORANGE FOREGROUND:
New territory is now available – Creative expression

MINOR ARCANA SYMBOLS-WANDS

WANDS PEOPLE

Wand people are Fire element; inspirational, growth-oriented, and ignited by Spirit.

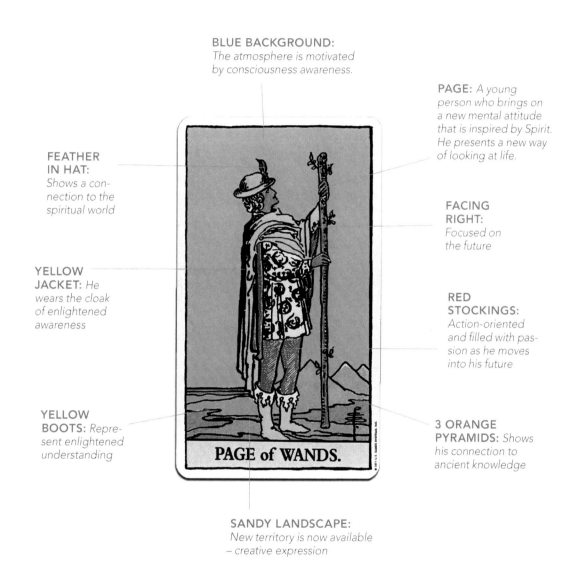

BLUE BACKGROUND: *The atmosphere is motivated by consciousness awareness.*

PAGE: *A young person who brings on a new mental attitude that is inspired by Spirit. He presents a new way of looking at life.*

FEATHER IN HAT: *Shows a connection to the spiritual world*

FACING RIGHT: *Focused on the future*

YELLOW JACKET: *He wears the cloak of enlightened awareness*

RED STOCKINGS: *Action-oriented and filled with passion as he moves into his future*

YELLOW BOOTS: *Represent enlightened understanding*

3 ORANGE PYRAMIDS: *Shows his connection to ancient knowledge*

SANDY LANDSCAPE: *New territory is now available – creative expression*

BLUE BACKGROUND:
The atmosphere is motivated by consciousness awareness.

ARMOR:
A symbol of protection that comes with having advanced to being a spiritual warrior.

PLUME: *Shows his connection is now protected by Spirit – The plume is of the Phoenix, the bird of transformation.*

SILVER BOOTS:
Enlightened understanding of the magnetic fields – An intuitive advantage

YELLOW JACKET:
He wears the cloak of enlightened awareness

PYRAMIDS: *Shows his connection to ancient knowledge that now includes personal experience and applied knowledge*

KNIGHT: *An action-oriented person who is a motivating force to move you to a new level in personal growth on your spiritual path.*

KNIGHT of WANDS.

SANDY LANDSCAPE:
Creative expression has advanced to include an enlightened foundation for living

TAPESTRY: *Represents her loyalty to life while living from the heart of passion and creativity.*

CROWN: *Symbol of authority.*

BLUE BACKGROUND: *The atmosphere is motivated by consciousness awareness.*

QUEEN: *A symbol of feminine authority. She has conquered the inner world and her presence shows us how we feel.*

WHITE CAPE: *Represents her ability to stay pure*

SUNFLOWER STAFF: *A symbol of being able to follow the light and have confidence*

LIONS: *The ability to stand tall in her kingdom and know she is protected.*

YELLOW DRESS: *Open to enlightened awareness.*

3 PYRAMIDS: *Shows her connection to ancient knowledge, includes a lightness of being.*

ORANGE SLIPPER: *Enlightened understanding of the magnetic and creative fields.*

BLACK CAT: *Indicates intuitive understanding and foundation for life. She has advanced her womanliness to independence.*

GREY THRONE: *The color of wisdom through integration*

MINOR ARCANA SYMBOLS—WANDS

TAPESTRY: *Represents his loyalty to life while living from the heart of passion and abundance.*

BLUE BACKGROUND: *The atmosphere is motivated by consciousness awareness.*

KING: *A symbol of masculine authority – He has conquered the outer world and his presence shows us how we think.*

CROWN: *Symbol of authority*

GREEN CAPE: *Shows his ability to manifest abundance that comes from his heart.*

LIONS: *Represents the ability to stand tall in his kingdom.*

RED ROBE: *Open to enlightened awareness through creative awareness and passion for life.*

SLIPPERS: *Enlightened understanding of the magnetic and dynamic fields.*

KING of WANDS.

SALAMANDER: *Represents the ability to live on the land and to live in the water.*

GREY THRONE: *The color of wisdom through integration*

MINOR ARCANA SYMBOLS–CUPS

CUPS

Cups symbolize the Water element and the Emotional plane. They connect you to your soul's expression of love and feelings. Cups speak to the depths of the emotional self, the heart's desire, how you love and are loved. Creative expression is resourced out of the Suit of Cups and brings forth fulfillment in life.

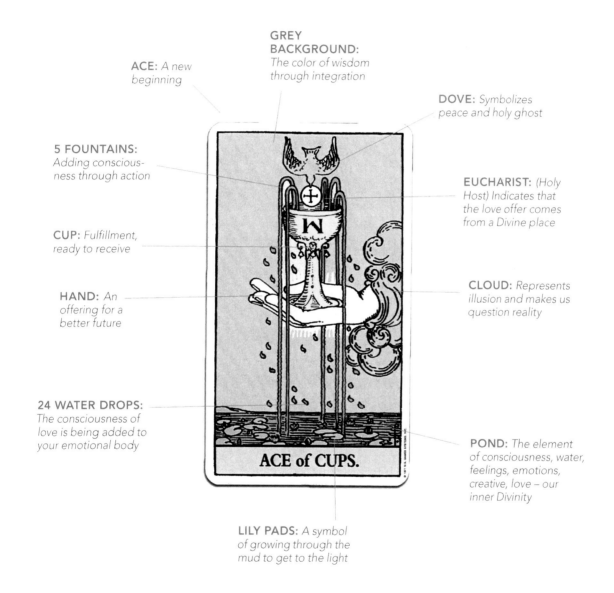

ACE: *A new beginning*

GREY BACKGROUND: *The color of wisdom through integration*

DOVE: *Symbolizes peace and holy ghost*

5 FOUNTAINS: *Adding consciousness through action*

EUCHARIST: *(Holy Host) Indicates that the love offer comes from a Divine place*

CUP: *Fulfillment, ready to receive*

HAND: *An offering for a better future*

CLOUD: *Represents illusion and makes us question reality*

24 WATER DROPS: *The consciousness of love is being added to your emotional body*

POND: *The element of consciousness, water, feelings, emotions, creative, love – our inner Divinity*

ACE of CUPS.

LILY PADS: *A symbol of growing through the mud to get to the light*

TWO: *Represents a coming attraction through balance and harmony.*

RED LION'S HEAD: *Fire energy at work here demonstrating the intention to be adored and to be loved*

BLUE BACKGROUND: *The atmosphere is motivated by conscious-ness awareness.*

RED WINGS: *Air element is in alignment with the love intention.* *All elements are present in this card indicating a unified field.*

CADUCEUS: *(Intertwined snakes) kundalini is present in their attraction – a merging of life forces*

RED & YELLOW JACKET: *Demon-strates a natural flow of passion and high-minded intelligence*

LAUREL LEAF CROWN: *A sign of victory*

BLUE SHAWL: *Shows that she is open to feelings and very receptive*

YELLOW STOCKINGS: *He walks the pathways of light*

WHITE DRESS: *Purity, virginity*

ORANGE/ YELLOW BOOTS: *Understanding is creative and passionate*

RED SHOES: *Shows Passionate understanding*

HILL & HOUSE: *A goal to be together in life will be actualized*

ORANGE FOREGROUND: *Creativity is at work here and holds the ground of being*

MINOR ARCANA SYMBOLS–CUPS

THREE: *Represents fun, creativity, being social, celebration*

BLUE BACKGROUND: *The atmosphere is motivated by consciousness awareness.*

FLOWERS IN HAIR: *Indicates that spiritual beauty has manifested and is their strength.*

DANCING: *A symbol of mastering the Earth plane*

WHITE ROBE: *Purity – a maiden*

ORANGE/WHITE ROBE: *A subtle opening to sensual awareness*

THREE GRACES: *Faith, Hope, and Charity*

RED ROBE: *Open to enlightened awareness through creative awareness and passion for life.*

BLUE SLIPPERS: *Receptive, intuitive awareness*

YELLOW SLIPPERS: *Enlightened awareness*

LANDSCAPE: *Fruitful and abundant, a reason to celebrate the gifts from life – harvest time*

ORANGE FOREGROUND: *Creativity is at work here and holds the ground of being*

FOUR: *Stability, structure, system*

TREE: *Roots are being set for a new foundation in love. Also known as the Tree of Happiness.*

BLUE BACKGROUND: *The atmosphere is motivated by consciousness awareness.*

GREEN ROBE: *Natural and willing to grow.*

FOURTH CUP OFFERED: *A new future of love is being offered – could miss it if he goes into illusion.*

RED SHIRT: *Open to enlightened awareness through creative awareness and passion for life.*

CROSSED ARMS & LEGS: *Body language shows that his heart is not open to receive the love that is being offered. There is a shutdown of the authority system.*

BLUE STOCKINGS: *Tendency for intuitive understanding and deeply sensitive.*

RED SHOES: *Passion is his pathway.*

GREEN MOUND: *A natural state of being*

MINOR ARCANA SYMBOLS–CUPS

GREY
BACKGROUND:
*Wise choices are
in the air*

FIVE: *Change,
variety, expansion*

BLACK ROBE:
*A sign of being deep
inside the void working
on the inner plane of
self-awareness*

CASTLE: *New
life and love can
be manifested*

BRIDGE:
*A connection be-
tween two worlds*

RIVER: *Flowing
toward a change
of consciousness*

FALLEN CUPS:
*Past love experiences
left behind due to lack
of fulfillment*

TWO CUPS:
*Indicate a decision
to love again*

YELLOW LANDSCAPE:
*Grounded enlightenment
is coming in*

SIX: *Love, commitment, home, health, happiness*

BLUE BACKGROUND: *The atmosphere is motivated by consciousness awareness.*

GREY ROOF: *Demonstrates that higher awareness is connected to wisdom*

YELLOW HOME: *The structure for living is happiness*

BLOND HAIR: *Strength is enlightened*

RED HOOD: *Passionate intention*

ORANGE/RED SCARF: *Creative, playful intention*

BLUE JACKET: *Indicates the intention of love and flowing feelings*

YELLOW BLOUSE: *Bright mind connected to the light*

RED KNEES: *Represent passionate authority*

WHITE GLOVE: *Indicates that she only knows purity – she is a virgin*

ORANGE STOCKINGS & BOOTS: *Symbolizes creative understanding*

BLUE DRESS: *Indicates love and feelings that are open and flowing.*

GREY GATE: *The family crest was designed with the family theme of integration and acceptance of combined blood lines.*

RED SLIPPER: *Her personal intention is passion with action – she is ready to act*

YELLOW FOREGROUND: *Indicates pure happiness coming from the Sun*

CUPS & DAISIES: *Happiness is a reality in the love exchange*

MINOR ARCANA SYMBOLS—CUPS

SEVEN: *Genius at work – learning lessons and getting smart*

RED AURA: *(over something hidden) Shows an experience of passion not yet experienced.*

BLUE BACKGROUND: *The atmosphere is motivated by consciousness awareness.*

HEAD IN CUP: *Represents a projection about someone he has feelings about.*

SNAKE: *A symbol of wisdom that comes with a transformation.*

CLOUDS: *Represent illusions*

DRAGON: *A symbol of enlightened speech, protection.*

CASTLE: *Represents a dream come true*

JEWELS: *Hidden treasure, opening to a new level of abundance that comes when you embrace the big picture.*

WREATH: *Symbolizes victory*

MAN: *(wearing black), a sign that inner work is in process*

EIGHT: *Manifestation of love*

BLUE BACK-GROUND: *The atmosphere is motivated by consciousness awareness.*

ECLIPSE: *A symbol of the end of a 19-year cycle*

ROCKS: *He is heading toward, and beyond, what has blocked him from getting what he wants.*

MAN: *Wearing Red – Represents taking action*

YELLOW STOCKINGS: *Indicate enlightened focus and intention*

RIVER: *(flowing downstream).His feeling are flowing and releasing so he can be free to manifest*

RED BOOTS: *Understanding action is necessary to manifest his true desire in love*

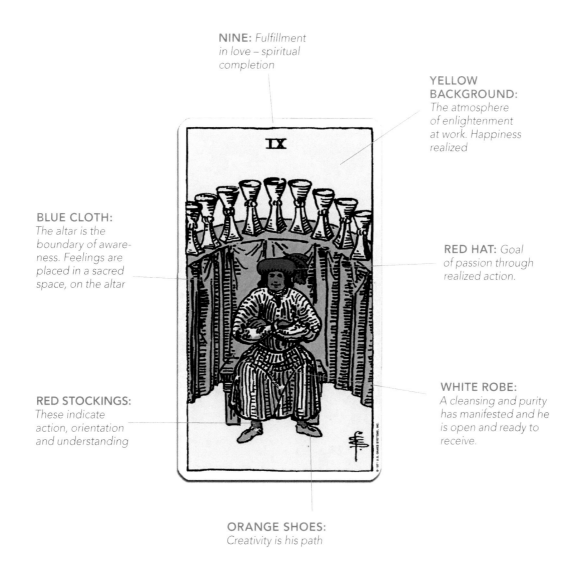

NINE: *Fulfillment in love – spiritual completion*

YELLOW BACKGROUND: *The atmosphere of enlightenment at work. Happiness realized*

BLUE CLOTH: *The altar is the boundary of awareness. Feelings are placed in a sacred space, on the altar*

RED HAT: *Goal of passion through realized action.*

RED STOCKINGS: *These indicate action, orientation and understanding*

WHITE ROBE: *A cleansing and purity has manifested and he is open and ready to receive.*

ORANGE SHOES: *Creativity is his path*

TEN: *New beginning in Love – love that lasts the test of time*

BLUE BACK-GROUND: *The atmosphere is motivated by consciousness awareness.*

RAINBOW: *Happy future is within sight*

RED & BLUE OUTFITS: *Shows that passion and feelings are integrating*

HOUSE & TREES: *A happy foundation is set and manifested.*

RIVER: *Indicates that consciousness is flowing their way.*

BOY/GIRL DANCING: *Symbolizes a happy future*

MAN/WOMAN: *Open and ready to receive*

ORANGE FOREGROUND: *Represents a creative foundation*

CUPS PEOPLE

Cups people teach us about feelings, creativity, and love.

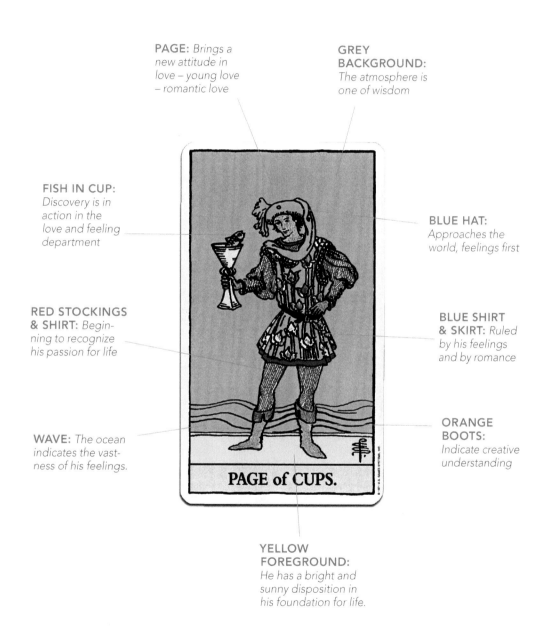

PAGE: *Brings a new attitude in love – young love – romantic love*

GREY BACKGROUND: *The atmosphere is one of wisdom*

FISH IN CUP: *Discovery is in action in the love and feeling department*

BLUE HAT: *Approaches the world, feelings first*

RED STOCKINGS & SHIRT: *Beginning to recognize his passion for life*

BLUE SHIRT & SKIRT: *Ruled by his feelings and by romance*

WAVE: *The ocean indicates the vastness of his feelings.*

ORANGE BOOTS: *Indicate creative understanding*

YELLOW FOREGROUND: *He has a bright and sunny disposition in his foundation for life.*

MINOR ARCANA SYMBOLS–CUPS

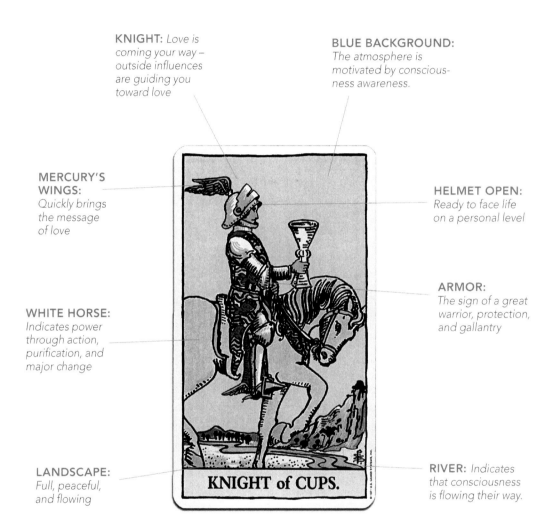

KNIGHT: *Love is coming your way – outside influences are guiding you toward love*

BLUE BACKGROUND: *The atmosphere is motivated by consciousness awareness.*

MERCURY'S WINGS: *Quickly brings the message of love*

HELMET OPEN: *Ready to face life on a personal level*

WHITE HORSE: *Indicates power through action, purification, and major change*

ARMOR: *The sign of a great warrior, protection, and gallantry*

LANDSCAPE: *Full, peaceful, and flowing*

RIVER: *Indicates that consciousness is flowing their way.*

KNIGHT of CUPS.

QUEEN: *A symbol of feminine authority, reflecting our emotional self, symbolizing our love nature and our feeling tone for life.*

CROWN: *Symbol of authority*

CROSS ON CHALICE: *Her domain is also the world – time infinite and time now*

FISH ON CHALICE: *Her domain is the ocean, the consciousness of dreaming, fantasy, and vastness*

BLUE SLIPPER: *Understanding is based on feelings*

BLUE BACKGROUND: *The atmosphere is motivated by consciousness awareness.*

GREY THRONE: *Supported by integration of all 4 worlds – She is seated on wisdom*

CHALICE: *Lid on it indicates that she is a vessel of love within herself, self-love. Able to contain her feelings and believes in the mystery*

WHITE GOWN, RED TRIM: *Represents purity, innocence and a bit of passion, on occasion.*

ANGELS ON THRONE: *She is connected to higher realms of awareness.*

SITTING AT TIDE: *Indicates her ability to flow in and out with her feelings and stay grounded.*

QUEEN of CUPS.

KING: *A symbol of masculine authority. His domain is the ocean, the vast consciousness of love and the depth of his feelings*

GREY BACKGROUND: *The atmosphere is motivated by wisdom and the ability to be open to new light, awareness.*

RED TRIMMED CROWN: *Symbol of potent authority*

GREY THRONE: *The color of wisdom through integration*

CUP & STAFF: *Shows his ability to receive and rule*

RED SCARF: *Potent passion*

BLUE ROBE: *Wearing his feelings*

YELLOW CAPE: *High level of an enlightened mind*

GREEN SLIPPERS: *Natural understanding of the magnetic and dynamic fields*

KING of CUPS.

WATERY LANDSCAPE: *Absence of firm ground; challenge of being grounded*

MINOR ARCANA SYMBOLS—SWORDS

SWORDS

Swords symbolize the Air element and the Mental plane. Swords can build you up or tear you down. They are double-edged, indicating the dualistic nature that exists in the mind. They teach offense or defense, encouragement or discouragement. Swords show where you are defining yourself and moving towards your own identity, or where you are giving power away to acquiesce to the needs of others. Swords ask you to have the courage to cut the apron strings on society and family and develop yourself as an individual. Swords are the motivational development of your personal power.

LAUREL & PALM BRANCHES: *Represents victory that comes in life by knowing and accepting yourself*

SIX YODS: *A Hebrew letter that indicates the Finger of God is pointing you in the right direction – six shows that the direction is Love*

CLOUD: *Illusion or a change of consciousness*

ACE: *A new beginning and opportunity*

CROWN: *A symbol of owning your own authority*

SWORD: *A symbol of the mind and its duplicity; it can build you up or destroy you.*

HAND: *A new future coming forward – an invitation for acceptance and personal definition*

GREY BACKGROUND: *The atmosphere is motivated by wisdom.*

BLUE & PURPLE MOUNTAINS: *Mountains are a symbol of attainment; the blue color is about mastering the feeling side of life while purple is about integrating the physical and spiritual aspects of life, thus, mastering life.*

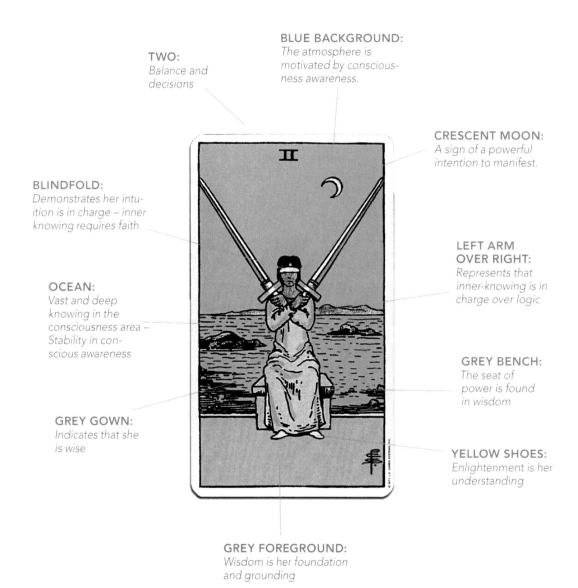

BLUE BACKGROUND:
The atmosphere is motivated by consciousness awareness.

TWO:
Balance and decisions

CRESCENT MOON:
A sign of a powerful intention to manifest.

BLINDFOLD:
Demonstrates her intuition is in charge – inner knowing requires faith

LEFT ARM OVER RIGHT:
Represents that inner-knowing is in charge over logic

OCEAN:
Vast and deep knowing in the consciousness area – Stability in conscious awareness

GREY BENCH:
The seat of power is found in wisdom

GREY GOWN:
Indicates that she is wise

YELLOW SHOES:
Enlightenment is her understanding

GREY FOREGROUND:
Wisdom is her foundation and grounding

MINOR ARCANA SYMBOLS–SWORDS

CLOUDS: *Illusion is confusing an issue and challenging self-esteem*

THREE: *Self, value, creativity, ego*

RAIN: *A change of consciousness is needed and happening now.*

SWORDS IN HEART: *Stress created from a loss of personal power, self-esteem challenges due to an outside influence playing ego games that hurt.*

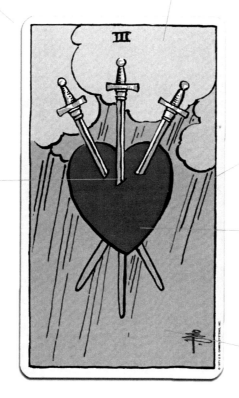

WOUNDED HEART: *Blocked ability to live love and flow with feelings*

GREY BACKGROUND: *The atmosphere is motivated by wisdom.*

FOUR: *Structure, organization, logic, systems*

STAINED GLASS WINDOW: *A new, more pleasant view of life is coming into reality by making the choice to say good-bye to soul sickness.*

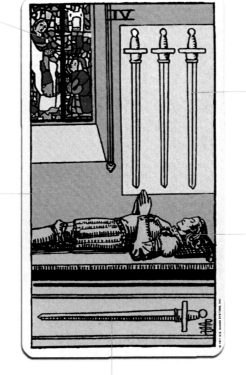

SWORDS ON WALL: *Indicates conquered past pain*

GREY BACKGROUND: *The atmosphere is motivated by wisdom.*

MAN ON COFFIN: *Represents the death of the ego.*

SWORD ON COFFIN: *Shows that a new identity is emerging – the ability to start over and move beyond past pain*

BLUE BACKGROUND: *The atmosphere is motivated by consciousness awareness.*

WIND-BLOWN CLOUDS: *Lots of mental activity in process.*

FIVE: *Represents change and expansion*

GREEN TUNIC: *He is now operating with a natural and balanced state of mind and is ready to go forward.*

RED HAIR: *(blowing in the wind) Indicates an overly active mind – Defensive thinking rather than thinking logically – Power struggles in his mind*

TWO MEN IN YELLOW: *(walking away) The battle of the mind is over; two mental aspects have left his mind.*

3 SWORDS: *Victory is achieved and self- esteem is built again through creativity.*

STORMY SEA: *Shows that a rough emotional process is stirring up emotions*

RED STOCKINGS & SHIRT: *Indicates that passion is dominate*

2 SWORDS ON GROUND: *Defense is no longer necessary – the cord has been cut.*

GREY FOREGROUND: *A foundation for learning has been established for wisdom to be applied.*

ORANGE BOOTS: *Indicate creative understanding*

GREY BACKGROUND: *The atmosphere is motivated by wisdom.*

SIX: *Love, home, family, health, happiness*

SMOOTH & ROUGH WATER: *Shows uncertainty about what's ahead, uncharted waters.*

MAN IN BOAT: *Mental aspects are in transition*

ALL 6 SWORDS IN BOAT: *Heading toward a more loving place to benefit the whole family.*

WOMAN IN BOAT: *Feeling aspects are in transition*

BOAT: *Symbolizes emotional balance*

CHILD IN BOAT: *Represents the desire to integrate and make a transition into wholeness.*

MINOR ARCANA SYMBOLS-SWORDS

YELLOW BACKGROUND:
Bright mind at work, leading to an enlightened awakening – a sign of happy days ahead

SEVEN:
Genius – getting smart

RED HAT:
Passion for his thoughts

BROWN SHIRT:
Action follows thought and leads to manifestation. Thus, struggle comes to those who use the mind without action.

2 SWORDS IN GROUND:
Indicate a decision has been made

5 SWORDS IN HANDS:
He is making a change in his thinking by expanding his thinking pattern.

CITY:
Symbolizes moving past an old way of thinking and going outside the box with new thoughts

GREY LEGGINGS:
Motivated by wisdom

RED BOOTS:
Understands success is a result of action

YELLOW FOREGROUND:
Sets the foundation for the bright mind to inspire awakenings.

MINOR ARCANA SYMBOLS-SWORDS

GREY BACKGROUND:
The atmosphere is motivated by wisdom.

EIGHT: *Money, power, success*

WOMAN IN RED:
*(bound and blindfolded)
A sign that there is an emotional aspect that is unable to accept what has already manifested. She is bound up from her inner rage due to mental exhaustion from perfectionistic attitudes that keep her from seeing what good she has done.*

8 SWORDS:
*(surrounding her)
Symbols of victory and success that she can't see – denial of success*

CASTLE: *Success has manifested*

WET, SANDY GROUND:
Lacking stability and understanding

BLACK BACKGROUND:
The atmosphere is motivated by a connection to the depth of the unconscious realm – in psychological terms, "being in the shadow self"

NINE: *Completion, spirituality, humanitarian, vulnerability due to being ultra-sensitive*

BLUE SWORDS ABOVE HEAD:
His mind has been captive to the emotional side of the mind and destructive thinking is in control – a sign of depression – only one point of view is available

MAN IN WHITE ROBE:
Purification in process – releasing pain

HANDS ON FOREHEAD:
Blocked vision based on fears and phobias taking over

BED:
Symbolizes the Ego

QUILT WITH FAMILY CREST:
Family issues are up for review

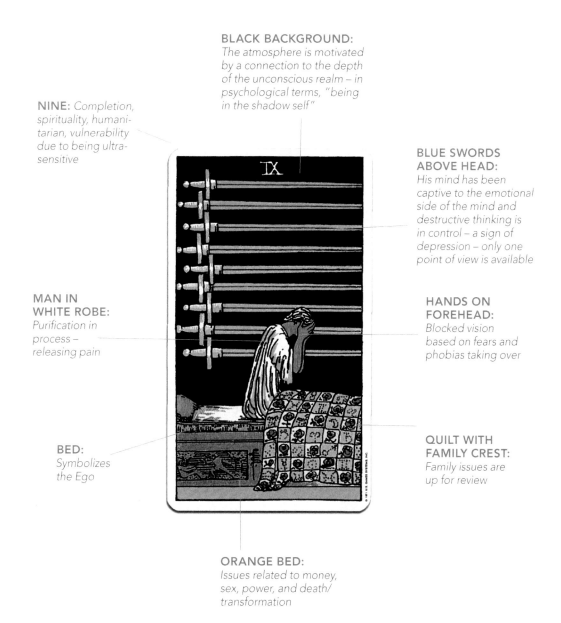

ORANGE BED:
Issues related to money, sex, power, and death/transformation

BLACK BACKGROUND: *The atmosphere is motivated by a connection to the depth of the unconscious realm – in psychological terms, "being in the shadow self"*

TEN: *New beginnings – future is set for success based on completing the learning cycle*

BLUE & WHITE SWORDS: *Logic and feelings have come into balance*

YELLOW HORIZON: *Sun is setting, the end of a cycle, the brighter side of the mind is opening to see the light*

BLUE MOUNTAIN RANGE: *Goal of the feeling side of the mind has been accomplished*

SMOOTH WATER: *(with brown streak) Feelings have been grounded in a new reality*

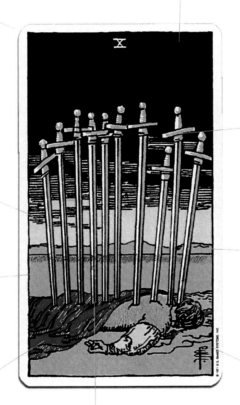

ORANGE SHIRT: *Creative power has returned*

RED BLANKET: *Comfort zone for passion has been realized and is in working order again*

10 SWORDS IN BACK: *The pain of the past is over, done and complete.*

MINOR ARCANA SYMBOLS—SWORDS

SWORDS PEOPLE

Sword people are all about getting smart. Their minds are what matters and they are recognized for their attainment and expression of knowledge.

PAGE: *A new mental attitude, a new generation of thought*

BLUE BACKGROUND: *The atmosphere is motivated by consciousness awareness.*

WINDY DAY: *Air element is activating the mind and its expression*

CLOUDS: *Illusion potential*

YELLOW LEGGINGS: *Enlightened action*

RED BOOTS: *Passionate understanding*

PAGE of SWORDS.

GRASS: *Natural foundation*

MINOR ARCANA SYMBOLS—SWORDS

KNIGHT:
Motivating force coming your way, super-charged thought waves

BLUE BACKGROUND:
The atmosphere is motivated by consciousness awareness.

WIND-BLOWN CLOUDS: *Moving beyond illusion*

RED SCARF:
Action required

WHITE HORSE:
Motivated by pure intention

HELMET:
(face mask up) Not at war. Peaceful state of mind

WINDY DAY:
Air element is activating the mind and its expression

ARMOR:
Protection is on its way

KNIGHT of SWORDS.

YELLOW & RED LANDSCAPE:
The ground-state is enlightened passion.

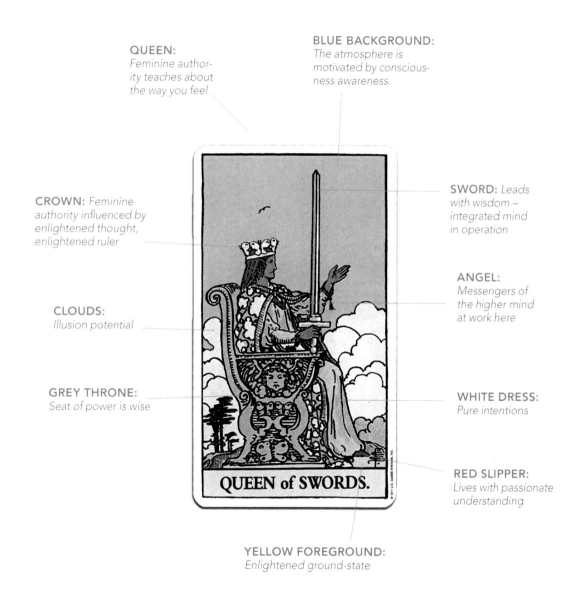

QUEEN:
Feminine authority teaches about the way you feel

BLUE BACKGROUND:
The atmosphere is motivated by consciousness awareness.

CROWN: *Feminine authority influenced by enlightened thought, enlightened ruler*

CLOUDS:
Illusion potential

GREY THRONE:
Seat of power is wise

SWORD: *Leads with wisdom – integrated mind in operation*

ANGEL:
Messengers of the higher mind at work here

WHITE DRESS:
Pure intentions

RED SLIPPER:
Lives with passionate understanding

QUEEN of SWORDS.

YELLOW FOREGROUND:
Enlightened ground-state

KING: *Masculine authority teaches about the way you think*

BLUE BACKGROUND: *The atmosphere is motivated by consciousness awareness.*

BACKDROP WITH BUTTERFLIES: *Wise connection to transformation*

CROWN: *Masculine authority influenced by enlightened thought – enlightened ruler*

RED SCARF: *Operates in the world with action and passion*

PURPLE CAPE: *Sign of a strong ego*

BLUE & GREY SWORD: *Integrated mind*

BLUE GOWN: *Wears his feelings openly*

RED SLIPPER: *Lives with passionate understanding*

CLOUDS *Illusion potential*

KING of SWORDS.

PENTACLES

Pentacles/coins symbolize the Earth element and Physical plane. They represent the field of abundance and your reaction to it and are related to self-value. The results in your life are commensurate to the way you value yourself.

GREY BACKGROUND:
The atmosphere is one of integration that leads to wisdom

ACE: New beginnings

CLOUDS:
Illusion potential

PENTAGRAM:
Represents man in his strongest position, a 5-pointed star formed by the head, two arms, and two feet, a symbol of direction and navigation

HAND:
An offering for a better future

MOUNTAIN PEAKS:
Suggests that accomplishment is available by making a choice to accept the peaks and valleys life offers when getting to a new level.

FENCE OF ROSES:
A boundary set for passion and action; a requirement of the earth element and the physical plane.

GARDEN OF LILIES: A setting for purity and peace

GRASS FOREGROUND:
The ability to accept the abundance in Nature

PATHWAY & ARCH:
An invitation to go beyond your comfort zone into an increase in abundance.

ACE of PENTACLES.

TWO: Balance and harmony; using polarity to manifest rather than being indecisive.

BLUE BACKGROUND: The atmosphere is governed by creative visualization – clarity of thought equals good manifesting ability

TALL RED HAT: Shows the expansion of thought coupled with a passionate intention to accept a new abundance package.

BALANCING COINS: Abundance is doubling based on keeping polarities in motion

INFINITY SYMBOL: Manifestation in motion

RED STOCKINGS & SHIRT: He is willing to take action to go for it and do what it takes to manifest

SHIPS: Clearly his "ships are coming in," good fortune is on its way, balanced emotions are important to create and accept abundance

GREEN SHOES: Understanding that his connection to Nature is necessary to manifest abundance.

WAVES: Shows the ability to flow with the energy required to manifest.

GREY FOREGROUND: Integrated wisdom – beyond judgement

THREE:
Creativity

BLACK BACK-GROUND: *The deepest part of the Soul is in operation*

ARCHWAY & COINS:
A sign to show that your creativity has value and is directly connected to your spiritual inspiration

GREY BRICKS:
Wisdom is being built here through wise communication

MAN & WOMAN:
(accepting offer) mental (man) and emotional (woman) integration is required in order to be creative and accepting of the abundance it brings

MAN: *Standing on bench, a symbol of a higher or more advanced mental authority anointing what has been created*

MULTI-COLORED OUTFIT: *Creativity comes from the feminine side of the mind*

GREY CHURCH FLOOR:
Ground of being is beyond judgement – integration

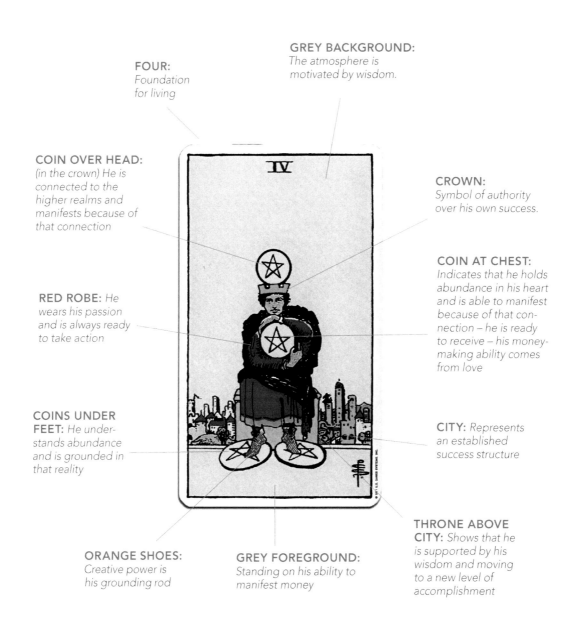

FOUR: *Foundation for living*

GREY BACKGROUND: *The atmosphere is motivated by wisdom.*

COIN OVER HEAD: *(in the crown) He is connected to the higher realms and manifests because of that connection*

CROWN: *Symbol of authority over his own success.*

COIN AT CHEST: *Indicates that he holds abundance in his heart and is able to manifest because of that connection – he is ready to receive – his money-making ability comes from love*

RED ROBE: *He wears his passion and is always ready to take action*

COINS UNDER FEET: *He understands abundance and is grounded in that reality*

CITY: *Represents an established success structure*

ORANGE SHOES: *Creative power is his grounding rod*

GREY FOREGROUND: *Standing on his ability to manifest money*

THRONE ABOVE CITY: *Shows that he is supported by his wisdom and moving to a new level of accomplishment*

BLACK & WHITE BACKGROUND: *Integration that brings about a change – imminent change is about to occur*

FIVE: *Change*

5 COINS IN WINDOW: *A new vision of abundance has arrived as a choice point, can choose abundance or lack*

MAN ON CRUTCHES: *A mental attitude that needs support to move forward*

WOMAN: *Forward motion is necessary*

ORANGE ROBE: *Her creativity is intact*

BLUE SHIRT: *He is wearing his feelings, they are not hidden – he is receptive to change*

SNOW: *Frozen consciousness*

BANDAGED FOOT: *Understanding has been compromised or it's healing*

GREY BACKGROUND: *The atmosphere is motivated by wisdom.*

SIX: *Love, family, service, home*

RED HAT & SCARF: *Shows manifestation abilities are active and flowing*

RED ROBE: *He wears his passion and is always ready to take action*

BLUE SHIRT: *Feelings are available for sharing*

COINS: *Sharing the wealth*

SCALES: *Holding the space for an equal exchange*

BEGGAR IN YELLOW: *Ready to receive and advance to a better state of mind*

BEGGAR IN BLUE: *Feelings are keeping him in the desperate zone. He's in victim-mode and has too much shame*

GREEN BOOTS: *Healthy understanding*

GREY FOREGROUND: *Wise ground-state*

GREY BACKGROUND: *The atmosphere is motivated by wisdom.*

SEVEN: *Getting smart – the mind*

PONDERING THE SIX COINS: *Pausing to contemplate, rather than completing*

ORANGE OVER-GARMENT: *Shows the ability to move forward in life*

BLUE UNDER-GARMENTS: *Represents that this is a man with compassion*

SEVEN COINS: *(six on the plant and one on the ground) The project is almost done; just one more step to go.*

MOUNTAIN PEAKS: *Symbolic of the peaks and valleys in life*

BOOTS: *The red boot in the water shows that he is motivated by his deep passion, while the brown boot on the land shows his understanding of the practical application needed to get the job done.*

GREY BACKGROUND: *The atmosphere is motivated by wisdom.*

EIGHT: *Money, power, success*

RED HAIR: *Represents strong intention towards action*

FIVE MOUNTED COINS: *An expansion has occurred. Shows us that manifestation comes only after action.*

BLUE SHIRT: *The heart of compassion is at work here and is in a creative flow.*

RED BOOTS & LEGGINGS: *Action is in place and run by pure passion*

CITY: *He has moved beyond the limits of his mind.*

YELLOW FOREGROUND: *More enlightened, support structure is connected with the Sun*

NINE: Completion, now ready for spiritual application to be transferred to physical reality

YELLOW BACKGROUND: The source of the Sun is the influence of power, happiness, and abundance.

TWO TREES: Working both ends of the polarity system (right/wrong, good/bad, woman/man, etc.) is necessary for manifesting – keeping balance

RED HAT: Shows that she is living the passionate life she intended – she's "working it"

FALCON: Bird-of-prey, not hunting but keeping the energy moving and her manifestation flowing – it's a happy hunting ground!

MOUNTAINS: A symbol of accomplishment on many levels

HOMES: The future is secure.

WOMAN'S DRESS: She wears her connection to light and happiness

WOMAN IN VINEYARD: Highly receptive to abundance

RED FLOWERS ON DRESS: The symbol of Venus (feminine principle) indicating passionate receptivity is necessary to manifest luxury

NINE COINS IN VINEYARD: Abundance has arrived – harvest will bring abundance

SNAIL: Indicates that the pathway is open to receive the gifts of her abundant garden

YELLOW FOREGROUND Indicates her ground of being is connected to enlightenment

TEN: *New beginnings – the future is here now*

PILLAR & ARCHWAY: *Structured wisdom opening to a new arena – gateway to success*

TEN COINS: *(encircling the entire card) Opportunities are all around, a legacy has been made; more money than can be spent by this generation, the fortune has longevity, money that will last forever, inheritance, winning the lottery*

TOWER: *Symbolizes a new approach to living with a bigger view for success*

DANCING COUPLE: *Shows a unified field of integrating success through the power of dancing, a symbol for mastery.*

VILLAGE: *Presents a new area of living and learning*

CHILDREN DANCING: *A sign that this success will last for future generations.*

GRANDFATHER IN GARDEN OF ABUNDANCE: *A sign that this success has longevity*

TWO DOGS: *Celebrating with the family. This success also benefits nature.*

PENTACLES PEOPLE

Coins people represent the different, increasing stages of abundance. They are concrete evidence of manifesting success.

PAGE: *Opening to a new avenue of abundance*

YELLOW BACKGROUND: *Open to the light and the source that comes from the Sun*

COIN IN HAND: *He is open to receive and is accepting the opportunity*

RED HAT & SCARF: *He intends to take action and stay in the flow, a new job/promotion/raise, new stage, new business*

GREEN OUTFIT: *He is in the natural flow of abundance.*

ORANGE BOOTS & LEGGINGS: *His ground of being comes from creative resources*

TREES: *Symbol of growth*

MOUNTAIN PEAK: *A goal will be accomplished*

MEADOW: *He is open to a wider formula for success*

PAGE of PENTACLES.

KNIGHT: *Abundance is on its way*

YELLOW BACKGROUND: *Open to the light and the source that comes from the sun. Happiness is here now*

FEATHER: *His connection to Spirit is active*

RED BRIDLE: *The concept of action and power has been realized*

HELMET: *(face mask up) He arrives in peace to receive abundance*

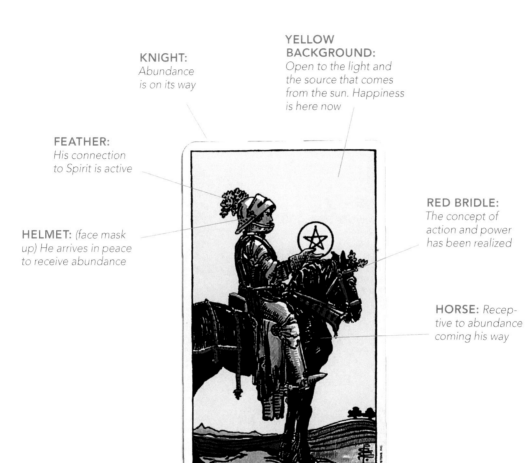

HORSE: *Receptive to abundance coming his way*

FIELD OF FURROWS: *Field has been tilled and the crop is growing – the work has been done and results are forthcoming*

YELLOW BACKGROUND: *Open to the light and the source that comes from the sun. Happiness is here now*

QUEEN: *Symbolizes receiving abundance*

RED FEATHERS: *Her passionate connection to Spirit has doubled her value*

ROSE ARCHWAY: *The Magician's intention has been realized.*

CROWN: *A symbol of her authority in the domain of abundance*

WHITE LILIES: *(etched on throne) Purity of intention is required in order to manifest*

COIN IN LAP: *Receptivity at its best*

QUEEN of PENTACLES.

MOUNTAINS: *Feelings are aligned with the accomplishment of the goal*

GARDEN IN BLOOM: *All of nature is expressing its abundance*

BULL ON THRONE: *Taurus, a symbol for abundance and manifestation*

GREY THRONE: *She sits on her wisdom knowing that the integration of opposites must happen in order to manifest.*

KING: *Highest level of abundance has been achieved and received*

YELLOW BACKGROUND: *Open to the light and the source that comes from the sun. Happiness is here now*

GOLD BULLS ON THRONE: *Taurus manifesting true value by being valuable*

STAFF WITH YELLOW ORB: *His domain of power comes directly from the Sun*

CASTLE: *A dream has come true*

MOUNTAINS: *Feelings are aligned with the accomplishment of the goal*

COIN IN HAND: *The future is set for the experience of great wealth*

GRAPES ON ROBE: *Represent total abundance*

GREY WALL: *Setting the boundaries to contain the wealth*

BLACK THRONE: *Symbolizes receiving at the deepest level*

KING of PENTACLES.

VINEYARD: *A symbol of fruition*

READINGS

Let the games begin. The fun starts here by using the oracle of the Tarot to discover all about yourself and your life. Get your questions ready. Ask for guidance to direct you toward one of the readings that interests you and the situations in your life. Be curious, have an open mind, and last but not least, have fun!

READINGS

PREPARING FOR A READING

Fan your cards face down on a table. Using the palms of both hands mix them well, turning them in various directions so they form a pool of conscious-ness "pool" in front of you. This form of mixing holds the energy in the cards and keeps your cards in better condition, while the standard form of shuf-fling should only be used to dispel negative energy from your cards.

Mixing can take anywhere from 10 seconds to 2 minutes or more. Stop mixing when you feel com-fortable with the energy exchange. The amount of time spent mixing the cards will probably vary each time you use them. Ask for guidance and direction while mixing the cards.

Now, you are almost ready to do your first reading. You might want to light a candle to focus the energy in the room before working with the cards and say a blessing, asking for information to be shown to you that will serve your highest and best purpose.

PULLING THE CARDS

It's important to note here that energy moves from left to right, just as our eyes do when we read. It is best to pull all cards face down, and keep them face down, while placing them in front of you in the sequence and design shown in the diagram for the specific reading you have chosen. This keeps you clear while pulling. If you turn the cards face up before completing the spread and prior to inter-pretation of the entire reading, you could be un-consciously influencing each succeeding card in the spread. After the cards are pulled from the "pool" and set in their appropriate places, turn each card over from left to right. In other words, the lower left corner of the face down card becomes the lower right corner of the face up card. Remember to always turn your cards over the same way for con-sistency. You are now ready to interpret each card according to its position in the layout.

REVERSALS

Reversals are cards that are upside down to you as you read the cards. This is true whether you are read-ing for yourself or for someone else since the cards are always laid out for the reader, the person interpreting the cards.

Do not give your power away to the reversed cards! Remember, the whole basis of life on earth is dualistic and requires you to face the downside of yourself as well as the upside. Do not place judgement on your-self for a reversed card. The reversal is merely show-ing you the inner place and inner work that is needed in your development. Do not use the Tarot to make yourself wrong. Use the Tarot to observe yourself.

ASKING QUESTIONS

Using the Tarot requires teamwork and synergy. The cards work off of your energy. Working with the Tarot requires inquiry and curiosity. Be willing to formulate your questions with care. Do not rush. Take time to develop your questions. Always pose your questions in the most positive way.

For example, let's look at issues relating to money. Your question may be, "Am I headed for financial di-saster?" However, that's not the way to ask the ques-tion. When you ask a fear-based question, the Tarot will show you your fear. A better approach might be: "What am I learning from money right now?", "What attitudes do I need to look at relating to money?", or "How can I enhance my financial situation?"

TYPES OF READINGS
- Bedtime Tarot Meditation
- A Card a Day
- General Information
- Yes/No Reading
- Daily Reading
- Weekly Forecast Reading
- Yearly Forecast Reading
- How to Get What You Want
- Money and you or Career and You or Relationship and You Reading
- Where am I Now?/Where am I Headed?
- Relationship Reading
- Personal Reading
- The Issue Reading
- Self-Transformation Reading
- Whole Self Profile Reading
- Nancy Drew Reading
- Dimensional Approach To Life Aspects

READINGS

BEDTIME MEDITATION

Pull one card before going to sleep. Hold the card in front of you. Take a few deep breaths and get in a relaxed position.

Close your eyes and take a journey deep inside yourself. In your mind, ask to be taken to a space called the edge of the Universe. This may be an ocean scene, a mountaintop, or a distant galaxy. Journey to this place in your meditative state and allow yourself to see what comes in.

Once you have arrived at your special place, ask to be shown your personal pool of consciousness or reservoir of knowledge. Let your inner vision be your guide to finding your pool of consciousness. It may show you the Milky Way, an ancient well, a reflecting pool, or a giant lake.

Then, ask that the pool be open to learning the system of the Tarot. Ask that this system, the Tarot, become available to you in knowledge. Let your inner vision see the transfer of knowledge come to you. When you feel comfortable with the filling of knowledge, in your pool, gently bring yourself back to your room and open your eyes onto the Tarot card you pulled before the meditation.

Ask your card for a special message. Be aware of the symbol on the card that popped out at you when you first opened your eyes. What might it mean to you? Are there any colors that strike you more than others? If so, what does that say to you? Check the mood or feeling tone that you get from the card. What might that reflect to you?

Write down these questions and answers in your journal before falling asleep. Then, thank your card for the information and place it under your pillow. Remember to keep your journal by your bed so that you can write down your dreamtime information upon waking in the morning.

A CARD A DAY

- A card a day is a wonderful way to learn the Tarot. I suggest pulling a card in the morning. One card is enough.

- Start by mixing your cards into a pool on your table.

- Ask out loud, "What do I need to know about today?"

- Pull the card you are most attracted to from the pool, face down.

- Then, turn your card over, from left to right.

- Look at it and see what it is telling you about your day. Write in your notebook what you feel it might be telling you.

- At the end of the day go back to your card and write your experience of the day relating it to your card.

- This is one of the best ways to learn the Tarot.

READINGS

GENERAL INFORMATION

This particular reading does not require a question, but gives you a picture of where you are right now.

Mix the cards in a pool, face down. Pull seven cards, one at a time, and place them face down in front of you in the layout shown below.

Once all cards are in place, turn them over until all are face up. Remember to always turn your cards over the same way for consistency. Interpret the meaning of each card.

CARD POSITION # & MEANING	ADDITIONAL DETAILS
1-The distant past:	Covers a time period of anywhere from 3 months to a year.
2-The past week:	Covers the past 7 days.
3-The immediate influence:	What you're dealing with now.
4-The challenge or block:	Relates to the immediate influence the card in position 3 in the present.
5-The environment:	Circumstances that surround you now (work, home, friends, family).
6-Several weeks into the future:	The unactualized potential.
7-Several weeks into the future:	Further unactualized potential.

READINGS

YES/NO

Formulate a question to be answered by this yes/no reading. Be sure to state your question clearly and in a positive manner.

For example:

"Is it a good idea to...?"

"Is it still an option for me to...?"

"Would it best behoove me to...?"

Do not add timing to your question. If you want answers regarding timing, go to a reading that specifically designates timing.

Ask your question while you are mixing the cards face down in front of you.

Pull them out of the "pool", face down, in the sequence shown in the layout below.

Once all cards are in place, turn them over in sequential order, until all are face up.

Remember to always turn your cards over the same way for consistency.

All "right-side-up" cards mean "yes," while reversed cards mean "no."

• YES = Open door policies. Right-side-up cards show you your "go" signs and positive action you can take.

• NO = Closed door policies. Reversed cards show you your blocks to having what you want or areas to improve or work on in order to turn the situation around to get what you want.

Total up the number of Yes cards and No cards.

Card in position 3 counts double and is the most potent card regarding your question.

If the count comes up 3-3, now is not the time to know your outcome. All of the facts may not yet be available. Work on the blocks to turn them around in your favor.

READINGS

DAILY

Mix your cards as usual and gather them into a stack.

Cut the deck into four stacks face down (as shown below).

Turn over the TOP CARD of each stack. The top card shows what you are bringing in to be worked on in that area for the day.

Turn over EACH STACK and look at the bottom card. The bottom card shows the motivating force behind the top card.

Physical   Mental   Emotional   Spiritual

READINGS

WEEKLY FORECAST

Mix the cards as usual, face down, into a pool.

Pull one card, face down, and place into the Sunday position, as shown in the layout.

Continue pulling one card at a time, face down, until there is one card for each day of the week.

Once all cards are in place, turn them over in sequential order, until all are face up.

Remember to always turn your cards over the same way for consistency.

Interpret the meaning of each card.

You may want to record this reading for an end-of-the-week review and/or for comparison with a daily journal.

Sunday   Monday   Tuesday   Wednesday

Thursday   Friday   Saturday

READINGS

YEARLY FORECAST

The purpose of this reading is to get an overview of each month's "theme." This reading is usually done at the beginning of each year, but it can be done at any time that you want to look at the remainder of the current year. After completing the reading and before returning the cards to the deck, record each card pulled for each month. You will be amazed by the accuracy of this reading.

| January | February | March | April | May | June |
| July | August | September | October | November | December |

GENERAL READING

Mix your cards face down forming a pool.

Pull one card for each month of the year (or each month remaining in the year) and lay them face down in the card layout shown above.

Once all cards are in place, turn them over in sequential order, until all are face up.

Remember to always turn your cards over the same way for consistency.

Interpret the meaning of each card.

MORE IN-DEPTH YEARLY FORECAST

Separate the Major Arcana cards from the Minor Arcana cards in your deck. Mix the Major Arcana pile face down.

Pull a card, one for each month, from the Majors and layout as shown above. Set aside the Major Arcana pile.

Mix the Minor Arcana pile and pulling one card for each month from the pool. Place the Minor Arcana card on top of the Major Arcana card. Keep both cards face down.

The interpretation of the Major Arcana card will give you the universal theme for each month.

The suit of the Minor Arcana card will pinpoint the area in which you will be focusing
(Wands – Spiritual; Swords – Mental;
Cups – Emotional; Pentacles – Physical).

Then, for an even more specific area of focus, interpret the Minor Arcana card.

READINGS

HOW TO GET WHAT YOU WANT

This reading defines the steps you need to take to get what you want.

Choose a Major Arcana card from your deck that represents what you want. For example, do you want a new direction in your life? Pick The Star card. Do you want to get married? Pick The Lovers card. Link up your goal to a Major Arcana card from your deck.

Keep your goal card out of the pile and mix the other cards as usual, face down.

Then, stop and mentally connect your goal card to your goal, asking the goal card to represent what you want to accomplish.

Place your goal card back in the deck, face down, and mix again.

When you feel ready, begin turning over cards one by one until you get to your goal card.

Keep all your cards in the order in which they came up. The cards that preceded your goal card describe to you what you need to go through to get your goal accomplished.

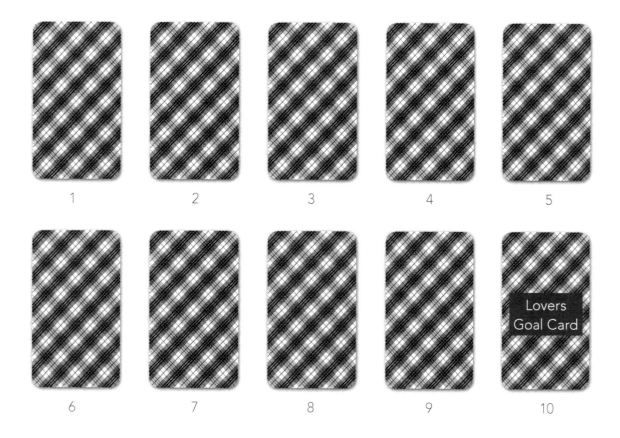

In this example, your goal is to get married, so you picked The Lovers card as your goal card. You pulled cards and laid them face up in the sequence until you got your goal card (The Lovers) on the 10th pull. You may pull many more cards until your reach your goal card or you may have to pull only a few.

READINGS

MONEY/CAREER/RELATIONSHIP & YOU

Choose an issue to work on for this reading.

Separate the Major Arcana cards from the Minor Arcana cards and turn the cards face down.

Mix the two stacks separately making two pools to draw from; one pool containing Minor Arcana cards, one pool containing Major Arcana cards.

First, pull from the Majors pool and place that card in position 1, as shown in Card Layout. Put the Majors stack aside.

Now, pull from the Minors pool for the rest of the reading and place Minors cards in positions 2, 3, 4, and 5.

Once all cards are in place, turn them over in sequential order, until all are face up.

Remember to always turn your cards over the same way for consistency.

Interpret the meaning of each card.

What I know
about the issue

Creative aspects
(of the issue)
available to me

Main Focus

How my thought
process relates
to the issue

Results I can
expect to produce
(or achieve)

READINGS

WHERE AM I NOW?/WHERE AM I HEADED?

Mix your cards in a pool face down.

You will pull five cards and lay them out as shown in card layout below. Ask each question out loud as you pull the card for that question, and place it in the layout face down.

For Position 1 ask: *Where am I now?* Place the card face down in position 1.

For Position 2 ask: *What is my next step?* Place the card face down in position 2.

For Position 3 ask: *Where am I headed?* Place the card face down in position 3.

For Position 4 ask: *What support am I getting from the Universe?* Place the card face down in position 4.

For Position 5 ask: *How does my environment support me?* Place the card face down in position 5.

Once all cards are in place, turn them over in sequential order, until all are face up. Remember to always turn your cards over the same way for consistency.

Interpret the meaning of each card.

Where I'm heading

Support I'm getting from the Universe (guides/teachers)

The next step

Support I'm getting from my environment

Where I am now

READINGS

ROMANTIC RELATIONSHIPS/COUPLES

Mix the cards, face down, in a pool in front of you.

Look at the statements by the positions in the card layout below. Pull each card, one at a time, as you say the statement for that position out loud.

Keep the card face down and place it into position according to the numbers shown in the card layout shown below.

Once all cards are in place, turn over the card in position 1 to show where you are in your process.

Turn over the card in position 2 to show where the other person is in his/her process.

Turn over the card in position 3 to see how you relate to the other person.

Turn over the card in position 4 to see how that person is relating to you.

Turn over the card in position 5, which shows the relationship as it stands right now and the process it is in. Relate card number 5 to all of the other cards.

This is the way I feel about the other person

This is the way the other person feels about me

The relationship as it stands now between me and the other person

This is where I stand right now in my process

This is where the other person stands right now in his/her process

READINGS

PERSONAL

Mix cards into the "pool."

Pull one card from the pool for each position.

As you select each card from the pool say out loud:

• This represents my (home, health, etc.) in the past.

• This represents my (home, health, etc.) in the present.

• This represents my (home, health, etc.) in the future.

Continue to work your way across each row.

Once all cards are in place, turn them over in sequential order, until all are face up.

Remember to always turn your cards over the same way for consistency.

Interpret the meaning of each card.

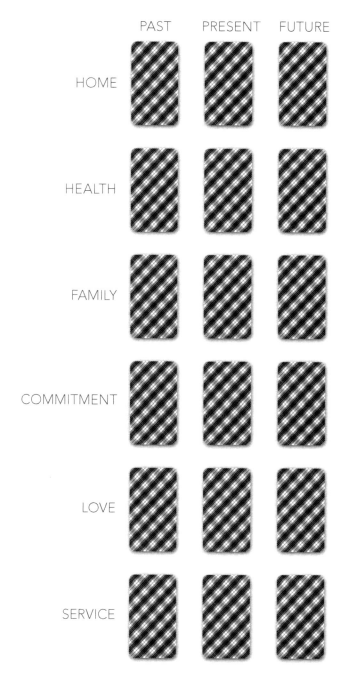

READINGS

THE ISSUE

Make a statement out loud about an issue. The more clearly you state your issue, the better the answer you will receive. Some examples: "My issue is my new car." "My issue is my money." "My issue is my relationship with (mother, father, boyfriend, girlfriend, children or any significant other)." "My issue is my work situation."

Mix the cards into a pool in front of you, face down.

Draw 10 cards, one at a time, and place them face down in sequence according to the positions, as shown below.

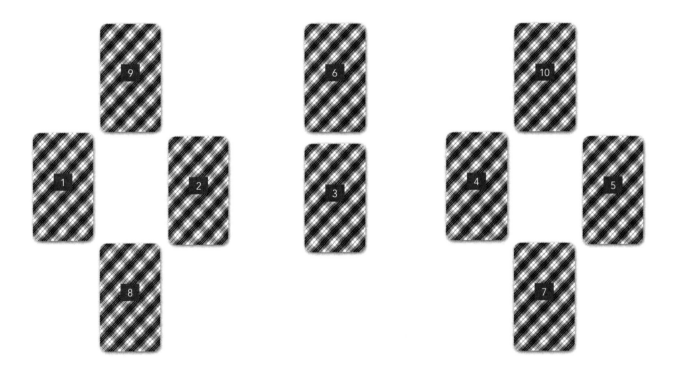

Once all cards are in place, turn the cards over one at a time in the following order:

Position 3: Represents you now

Position 6: Represents the real issue – This might appear different than what you asked. If it does, it represents the core issue from the subconscious.

Position 7: Represents what distracts you – Could be an outside influence or an aspect within yourself that keeps you from focusing on your issue.

Position 8: Represents what helps you – Could be an outside influence or an aspect within yourself of which you are unaware.

Position 9: Old focus[*]

Position 1: Older focus[*]

Position 2: Oldest focus[*]

Position 4: New focus[**]

Position 5: Newer focus[**]

Position 10: Newest focus[**]

[*]All three cards labeled old (-er, -est) focus represent where you came from.

[**]All three cards labeled new (-er, -est) focus represent where you are going with this issue and its, as yet, unactualized potential.

READINGS

SELF-TRANSFORMATION

Mix your cards as usual and ask each question out loud while pulling one card for each area.

Once all cards are in place, turn them over in sequential order, until all are face up. Remember to always turn your cards over the same way for consistency.

Interpret the meaning of each card as it relates to the question in that position in the layout.

1	2	3	4
What are my faults?	What are my virtues?	Where am I insecure?	Where do I value myself?

5	6	7	5
What am I denying?	What do I accept about myself?	What are my expectations?	What is my reality?

READINGS

WHOLE SELF PROFILE

This reading provides a profile of your wholeness and allows you to see your most positive characteristics in each category, as well as defining areas you need to work on.

Mix the cards into a pool face down.

Pull one card from the pool for each area defined below. When pulling a card say, "This represents me and my"_____(i.e., me and my identity, me and my intuition, etc.).

Place a card, face down, in each of the positions in the layout shown.

Once all cards are in place, turn them over in sequential order, until all are face up. Remember to always turn your cards over the same way for consistency.

Interpret the meaning of each card as it relates to the positions labeled in the card layout.

1	2	3	4	5
IDENTITY	INTUITION	FUN/CREATIVITY	SUCCESS	CHANGE

6	7	8	9	10
LOVE	LESSONS	MONEY	SPIRITUALITY	FUTURE

READINGS

NANCY DREW

There are times when you want to use the Tarot to discover where you are right now. This reading defines the area in which you need to focus your attention at the present time.

Choose a personality card (King, Queen, Knight or Page) that you are drawn to right now. It can be from any of the four suits. Get a feeling for it, remember it, place it back in the deck and mix the cards as usual.

Gather the cards (face down) into a stack.

Place the cards face down one at a time working your way from position 1 through position 10. Continue in this manner (from top of stack, face down, into positions 1 through 10), stacking the new row of cards on top of the previous row of cards until you have placed all the cards in the deck.

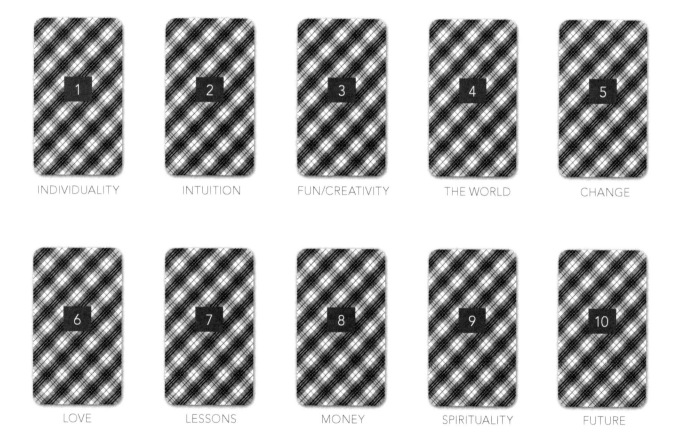

1	2	3	4	5
INDIVIDUALITY	INTUITION	FUN/CREATIVITY	THE WORLD	CHANGE

6	7	8	9	10
LOVE	LESSONS	MONEY	SPIRITUALITY	FUTURE

Look through each stack separately to find the personality card you were originally drawn to. The stack in which you find it represents the area on which you need to focus.

Move all other stacks out of the way.

Lay out the cards in the focus stack (face up) in a row, from left to right keeping them in the original order and interpret each card as it relates to the area.

READINGS

DIMENSIONAL APPROACH TO LIFE ASPECTS

This reading shows how you are handling the following life aspects on all four levels (spiritual, mental, emotional, and physical):

• Personality • Profession • Emotions • Environment
• Relationships • Health • Finances

| PERSONALITY | PROFESSION | EMOTIONS | ENVIRONMENT |
| RELATIONSHIPS | HEALTH | FINANCES | FUTURE |

Mix cards as usual.

Gather cards face down, into a stack.

Working from left to right, lay four cards (face down) in each position in the first row (positions 1-4) according to the card layout diagram.

Again working from left to right, lay four cards (face down) into each position in the second row (positions 5-8) of the card layout.

• The first card down, touching the table, is the Physical level of that aspect

• The second card placed on the stack is the Mental level of that aspect

• The third card placed on the stack is the Emotional level of that aspect

• The fourth card placed on the stack, the top card, is the Spiritual level of that aspect

Turn the cards over, either one card at a time, or by turning over the entire stack. Either way, the cards keep their same level assignments. The card that was touching the table is interpreted according to the Physical level and so on.